Trient Press®

Trient Press
3375 S Rainbow Blvd
#81710, SMB 13135
Las Vegas,NV 89180

Ordering Information:
Quantity sales. Special discounts are available on quantity purchases by corporations, associations, and others. For details, contact the publisher at the address above.
Orders by U.S. trade bookstores and wholesalers. Please contact Trient Press: Tel: (775) 996-3844;  or visit www.trientpress.com.

Printed in the United States of America

Publisher's Cataloging-in-Publication data
Trient Press
A title of a book : Trientrepreneur

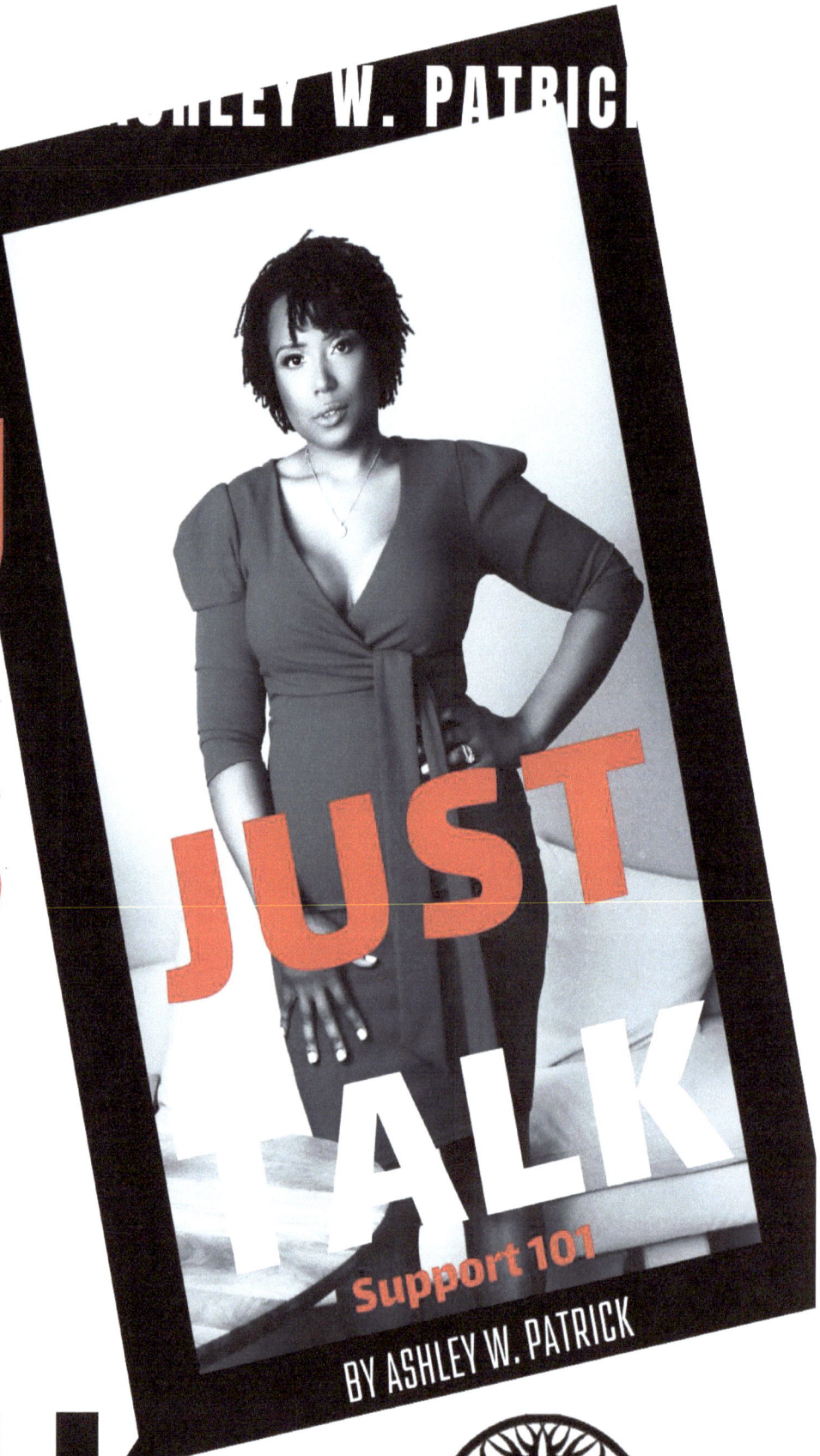

JUST

TALK

JUST TALK

Support 101

BY ASHLEY W. PATRICK

Trient Press®

TRIENTREPRENEUR

ISSUE 15

# TABLE OF CONTENTS

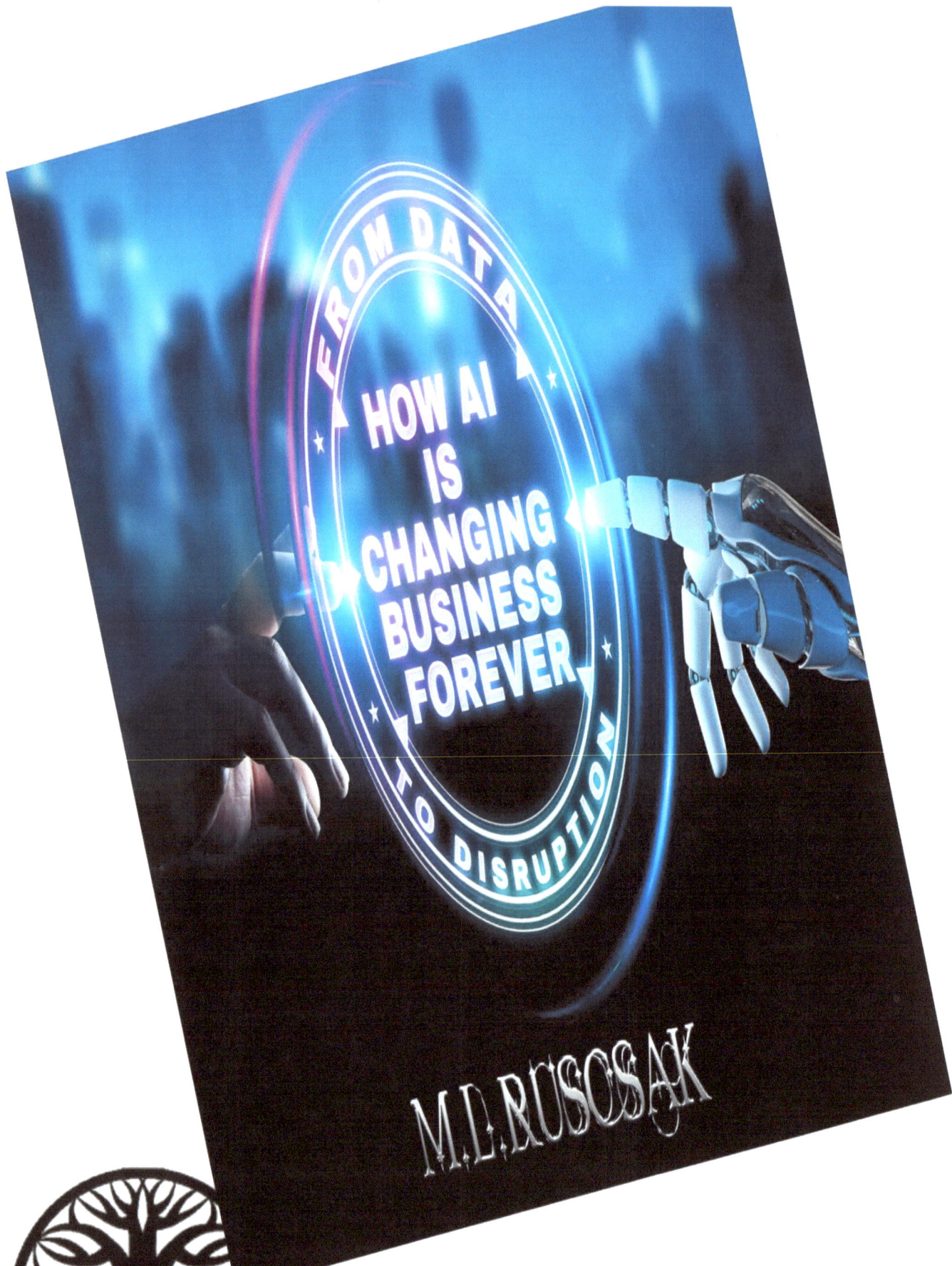

FROM DATA

HOW AI
IS
CHANGING
BUSINESS
FOREVER

TO DISRUPTION

M.D. ROSOSAK

Trient Press®

# AUTHOR TIPS: TOUCHDOWN WRITING

## 10 Authorship Lessons Inspired by the NFL Playbook

- **Team Collaboration:** Just as NFL teams thrive on teamwork, authors can benefit from collaborating with editors, designers, and marketers to bring their work to its highest potential.

- **Practice and Preparation:** Like athletes honing their skills, authors should practice their craft regularly and prepare by researching and outlining before diving into writing.

- **Resilience in the Face of Rejection:** NFL players face setbacks, and authors can learn to handle rejection by persistently submitting their work and refining their approach based on feedback.

- **Continuous Learning:** Just as NFL teams study their opponents, authors should continually read and analyze diverse content to expand their knowledge and style.

- **Strategic Goal Setting:** Similar to setting game plans, authors benefit from setting clear writing goals, such as word count targets or completing chapters by specific dates.

- **Feedback Utilization:** NFL players and authors both improve by learning from constructive criticism, using it to refine their skills and enhance their output.

- **Adaptability and Innovation:** Authors, like NFL teams, should adapt to changing trends and embrace innovative writing techniques to keep their content fresh and engaging.

- **Strong Opening Hooks:** As NFL games begin with captivating plays, authors should hook readers from the outset with compelling openings that ignite curiosity.

- **Consistent Performance:** Just as NFL players need consistent performance, authors should establish a writing routine to maintain steady progress.

- **Celebrating Milestones:** Authors can celebrate completing drafts or publishing achievements, mirroring how NFL teams commemorate victories and milestones.

THE ONE & ONLY UNCLE ME'SHORN

# I AM NOT YOUR BLACK, AMERICA

Me'Shorn T Floyd Daniels

Trient Press®

# BEHIND THE SCENES:

## The Economics of the NFL Empire

NEWS PROVIDED BY: Trient Press

—EACH FINDS ITS VALUE INSCRIBED IN DIGITS OF STAGGERING MAGNITUDE.

In the hallowed arena where the clash of titans unfolds, an empire emerges not solely defined by the riveting plays and mesmerizing athleticism that enraptures millions. This empire, cloaked in the splendor of the National Football League, is a microcosm of a vast economic tapestry that weaves together ambition, spectacle, and the ceaseless currents of commerce.

Venture beyond the roar of the crowd, the thrill of touchdowns, and the balletic prowess of athletes, and you'll find a meticulous architecture of economics underpinning the NFL's grandeur. Behind the scenes, an intricate symphony of transactions and strategies orchestrates this dynamic spectacle, producing a theater of not only physical prowess but also financial significance that reverberates on a global stage.

The fiscal ballet begins with franchise valuations, where teams metamorphose into corporate entities of substantial net worth. The perennial contenders, the storied underdogs

Broadcast rights, a veritable economic cornerstone, elevate the NFL's stature beyond national borders. The drama of contract negotiations, drafted with utmost precision, underscores the intricate dance between player earnings and team budgets. Here, the virtuosic plays on the field find their reflection in the art of financial negotiations.

Beyond the realm of athletes, the NFL's economic embrace extends like a symphony's crescendo, encompassing a constellation of industries. Picture the pilgrimage of fans—each adorned in team colors, hearts ablaze with anticipation—converging upon the coliseums of modernity. In their wake emerges a phenomenon that transcends sport, summoning a surge of travel, hospitality, and commerce. Host cities, once mere geographical coordinates, transform into bustling epicenters of financial vigor, their streets alive with the cadence of enthusiastic footsteps and the resonant pulse of transactions.

Here, the fervor of fandom is the catalyst that transforms the essence of the game into an engine of economic propulsion. Hotels burgeon with guests, eager to be in proximity to the unfolding drama. Restaurants, cafes, and eateries overflow with patrons seeking sustenance, discourse, and shared experience. An economy of experiences blossoms as cultural exchange intertwines with the resounding chorus of cheers.

exposure and credibility. By collaborating with influencers who have a strong following and align with their genre or target audience, authors can tap into existing communities and gain access to new readers. Whether through book reviews, interviews, or joint promotional efforts, influencer marketing can significantly amplify an author's reach and boost book sales.

Social media platforms have become indispensable tools for authors to connect directly with readers, build relationships, and generate buzz around their work. From sharing book updates to behind-the-scenes glimpses into the writing process, authors can leverage platforms like Instagram, Twitter, and Facebook to engage with their audience, host giveaways, and collaborate with influencers or fellow authors to expand their reach.

### Influencer Marketing:

Partnering with influencers and industry experts can provide authors with valuable

In the digital age, strategic marketing techniques are vital for authors to cut through the noise and connect with readers on a meaningful level. By building a strong author platform, creating valuable content, leveraging social media, collaborating with influencers, and harnessing the power of email marketing, authors can maximize their reach, amplify their brand, and achieve long-term success. Embracing these strategies in the ever-evolving digital landscape can position authors for growth and recognition in the highly competitive publishing industry.

Creating valuable content is a powerful way to attract and engage readers. Beyond writing books, authors can leverage various content formats such as blogs, articles, podcasts, and videos to provide insights, share expertise, and connect with their target audience. By consistently delivering high-quality content that resonates with readers, authors can establish themselves as thought leaders and foster a loyal following.

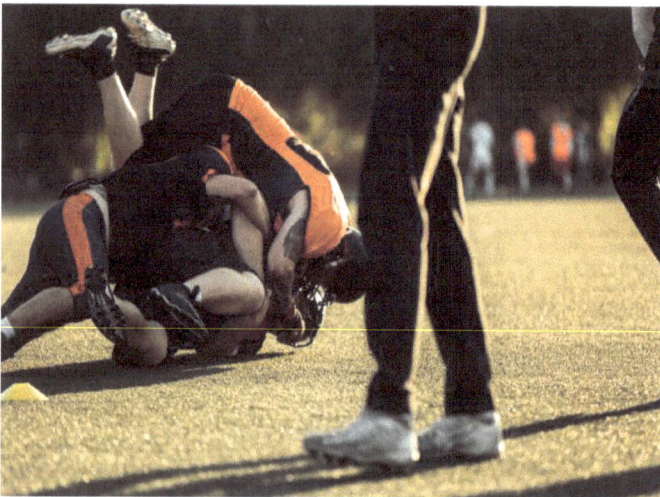

Yet, beyond the local tapestry, the NFL's allure casts a global net, drawing advertisers and sponsors into its orbit. Their presence, an eloquent ballet of imagery and message, sewn seamlessly into the seams of the game, becomes integral to the very fabric of the NFL's narrative. In this dance, brand narratives converge with the rhythm of touchdowns and tackles, creating an alchemy where commerce and competition coalesce.

As the saga of each season unfolds, we find ourselves at the confluence of economics and emotion. Ticket sales cease to be transactional entries; they evolve into tokens of shared belonging, entitling their bearers not just to a seat, but to an immersive experience woven with the threads of tradition and camaraderie. The games, often mere athletic contests, metamorphose into collective experiences—a modern-day rite transcending divisions, uniting communities in a shared crescendo of elation and heartache.

Then, there is the grand crescendo of them all—Super Bowl Sunday. A day of cultural gravity that stretches far beyond the confines of the stadium, encompassing living rooms, pubs, and gatherings across the globe. The resonance of this day, a testament to collective engagement, elevates commercials from mere marketing interludes to heralded moments of cultural significance. Brands step onto this grand stage not merely as sponsors, but as co-authors of a narrative etched into the annals of popular culture.

And so, behind the scenes, beyond the well-trodden gridiron and the jubilation of victory, the NFL Empire unfurls a panorama as intricate as a masterwork's brushstrokes. Here, economics and the ethereal dance of human emotion intertwine. It is an ode to how sport—this art—skillfully navigates the currents of capitalism. In doing so, it becomes an emblem, a resonant symbol of an empire where the alchemy of economics is as vibrant and evolving as the plays that etch themselves indelibly into our collective memory.

# From Draft Day to IPO: Lessons in Strategy from the NFL and Wall Street

In the grand tapestry of modern enterprise, where the dance of athleticism collides with the symphony of finance, a riveting narrative unfolds at the juncture of the NFL and Wall Street. Here, the journey from draft day to the initial public offering (IPO) becomes more than a mere sequence of events; it is a chronicle of strategic brilliance that reverberates through the corridors of both fields.

The juxtaposition of the NFL draft and the nascent stages of a startup venture may appear, on the surface, as a curious pairing—distinct arenas bound by disparate narratives. Yet, as the layers are gently peeled away, an exquisite symmetry emerges, a shared rhythm that underpins both realms. It is a rhythm that reverberates with a meticulous selection process, an unwavering devotion to potential, and the deliberate sculpting of a foundation from which future triumphs will bloom.

Within the hallowed realm of the NFL, the draft is a moment of resurgence, an annual occurrence where teams, both established and burgeoning, breathe life into their aspirations. This life breath—this audacious endeavor to align aspiration with potential—resonates in each name that is announced, in every athlete scrutinized for the promise they bear. It's a symphony of strategy, a ballet of anticipation, as teams gaze beyond the immediate horizons, seeking not just the instant gratification of a single play, but the harmonious alignment of prowess with a future that stretches like an open field.

And so, the startup embarks on a parallel journey. The inception of an enterprise mirrors the NFL draft in its meticulous selection process, one that culminates in the identification of founding members whose potential and passion align with the grandeur of their vision. The architecture of a startup is intricately woven, the foundation set with the recognition that its composition will profoundly shape the trajectory ahead. In this pursuit, the NFL's draft strategy, where immediate needs are deftly balanced against the horizon of sustained growth, finds its twin in the savvy of the visionary entrepreneur, orchestrating a trajectory that mirrors the ascent of an NFL star.

Yet, venture beyond the realm of selection and gaze upon the negotiation table. Here, the art of deal-making intertwines with the heartbeat of ambition, creating an arena that draws parallels between NFL athletes and the aspiring startups. In the delicate choreography of contracts, bonuses, and performance incentives, the narrative parallels the symbiotic dance between startups and venture capitalists. Potential meets prudence, aspiration interlocks with investment, and the negotiation table becomes a crucible where dreams intertwine with the pragmatism of calculated resource deployment.

And yet again, we pivot to the playbook—a term familiar both to NFL strategists and burgeoning business visionaries. Within the pages of the NFL playbook lies a treasury of plays, each meticulously designed for tactical advantage, but more profoundly, each thread woven into a broader narrative. Each play, every strategic maneuver, feeds into a larger symphony of strategy, one informed by past trials, tailored to exploit the chinks in the opposition's armor, and adaptive in the face of real-time evolution. The playbook is a testament to the culmination of wisdom, experience, and the nimble responsiveness that the game demands.

This symphony of strategy finds its harmonious echo in the startup's strategic blueprints. As startups embark on their own odyssey, each strategic maneuver forms a vital note in the melody of their narrative. Startups, much like NFL teams, cultivate a roadmap that draws from meticulous planning while remaining receptive to the improvisation that the dynamic landscape of reality demands. Just as NFL strategists pivot based on real-time game flow, startups adapt their trajectories to seize emergent opportunities, innovating not merely through design but through dexterous adaptation to changing circumstances.

**In the harmonious dance between the NFL's draft and the inception of startups, a shared rhythm emerges—a symphony of potential harnessed, strategies sculpted, and the delicate interplay of negotiation and ambition. It's a cadence that unites the field and the boardroom, revealing the universal melody of success composed through careful selection, strategic choreography, and the resonant balance of vision and pragmatism**

In this juxtaposition between the NFL draft, negotiation intricacies, and strategic playbooks, a profound symphony of parallels emerges. It's a symphony that traverses realms yet finds resonance in shared strategies, a rhythm that underscores the synergy of potential and ambition, negotiation and investment, and the intricate choreography of strategy. It speaks to the enigmatic dance between aspiration and pragmatism, potential and resource, strategy and adaptation. Ultimately, it unveils the universal cadence of success—one that reverberates through the hallowed fields of the NFL and resonates in the corridors of burgeoning businesses, a rhythm that echoes across time, united in its pursuit of excellence.

Now, enter the IPO—a crescendo of anticipation that echoes the Super Bowl's climactic moments. Just as NFL teams vie for the championship ring, startups vie for that ultimate validation—a public listing. The IPO, akin to the grand finale, represents a culmination of relentless efforts, exhaustive preparation, and an intricate choreography of timing.

The parallels between Wall Street and the NFL's complex negotiations run deeper still. The NFL's collective bargaining agreements exemplify the delicate interplay between diverse stakeholders—a symphony conducted for the greater good. Similarly, on Wall Street, IPOs necessitate the orchestration of regulatory bodies, underwriters, investors, and corporate visionaries in a harmonious ensemble.

As we traverse the landscape of these shared strategies, it becomes evident that the NFL and Wall Street aren't disparate territories; they're two sides of the same coin, each informed by a relentless pursuit of success through strategic acumen. Just as an NFL coach crafts plays for every conceivable situation, entrepreneurs draft business strategies that navigate uncertainty. The resounding success of both lies in the ability to seize opportunities, adapt to challenges, and cultivate a spirit that is indefatigably resilient.

In the ultimate synthesis, the NFL's playbook is much like Wall Street's strategic playbook. It's a symphony of tactics, a dance of negotiation, and a saga of calculated risk-taking. The journey from draft day to IPO—a journey of grit, strategy, and triumph—uncovers the intertwined DNA that underpins both these arenas. It serves as a testament to the boundless power of strategic thinking, where disparate fields find resonance in the pursuit of excellence.

"Like the crescendo of anticipation that heralds a Super Bowl's climax, the IPO stands as a grand finale—an intricate tapestry woven from relentless efforts, meticulous timing, and boundless preparation. Just as NFL teams vie for the championship ring, startups aspire for that ultimate validation—an entry onto the public stage. In this convergence of Wall Street's intricate negotiations and the NFL's collective harmony, we witness a symphony orchestrated for success, where diverse stakeholders coalesce for a greater purpose. Through the pages of history, both Wall Street and the NFL reveal themselves as twin pillars of strategic acumen, unified by an unwavering pursuit of triumph in the face of uncertainty. Their success resonates in the audacity to seize opportunities, navigate challenges, and cultivate a spirit that stands undaunted in the face of adversity. As we traverse this landscape of shared strategies, we discover that the NFL's playbook and Wall Street's strategic playbook are but chapters of the same narrative—an intricate dance of tactics, negotiation, and calculated risk. From draft day's inception to IPO's crescendo, a journey of resilience, strategy, and triumphant orchestration unveils itself, a testament to the unbounded power of strategic thought and the symphony of excellence that binds seemingly distinct fields in an eloquent pursuit of greatness."

TRIENT PRESS MAGAZINE

NFL EDITION

# The Economics of Game Day:
## Revenue Streams Beyond Ticket Sales

In the theater of sport, where the roar of the crowd and the clash of titans entwine, a profound economic symphony resounds, expanding well beyond the perimeters of the stadium. While the palpable excitement of game day echoes through the grandstands, it's the symphony of revenue streams—subtle and intricate—that orchestrates an economic ballet transcending the boundaries of the arena.

Amid the exhilaration of the NFL's game day, where fan fervor converges with team strategies, a multifaceted tapestry of revenue sources takes center stage. Ticket sales may be the initial refrain, but they are just the overture to a diverse and harmonious arrangement of financial dynamics. Beneath the iconic helmets and jerseys lies a microcosm of commerce—a synthesis of fan engagement, media exposure, and strategic partnerships that collectively form the heartbeat of the NFL's economic ecosystem.

The omnipresent allure of the televised spectacle fuels a remarkable dance of advertising and media rights. As the game unfolds, millions of eyes are drawn to the screen—a captive audience for advertisers seeking to align their narratives with the unscripted drama of the gridiron. The halftime show, a transcendent interlude, becomes a prime real estate for marketing, capitalizing on its mesmerizing allure to showcase new products, services, and brands. This intersection of sports and commerce transforms the NFL into a pulsating marketplace where advertisers vie to weave their stories into the narrative fabric of game day.

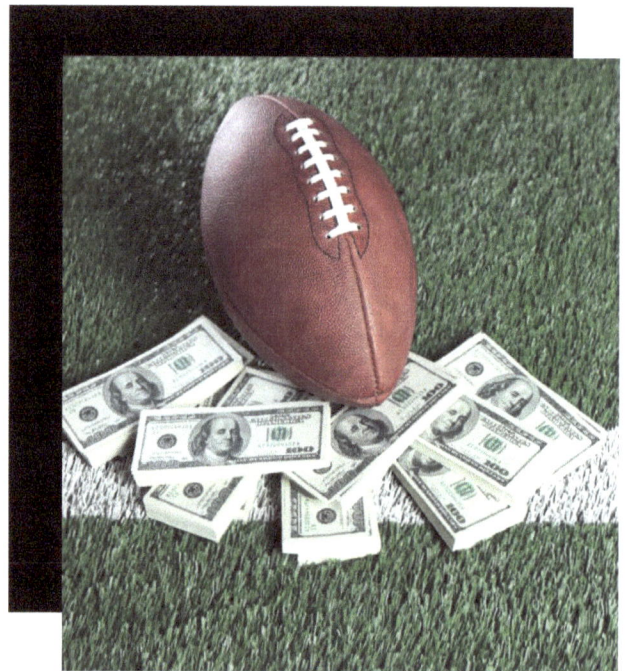

Beyond the screen, where the televised spectacle unfolds, the phenomenon of merchandise sales emerges as an indispensable cadence within the symphony of economic dynamics. The echoes of the crowd's roar reverberate through every jersey that bears the name of revered players, every hat and scarf emblazoned with team insignias. This tapestry of merchandise isn't just about ownership—it's a tangible connection, a bridge that spans the distance between fans and their cherished teams. This connection, woven through the threads of fabric and embroidered designs, takes on profound significance. It's more than a piece of clothing; it's a declaration, a visual anthem of allegiance. Enthusiasts don the colors of their team with pride, a proclamation etched in fibers that proudly binds their identity to the spectacle of the game. The intertwining of sports and commerce is evident here, where the act of wearing becomes a powerful symbol of shared passion, a testament to the deep-seated intimacy that marries the heart of the game to the currents of commerce.

## NFL Revenue Streams

•Should the NFL focus on all three revenue streams , a combination of the three, or just one?
•Which revenue stream stands to have the biggest gain from international expansion?

Yet, in the symphony of revenue streams, even the culinary offerings of game day carve out a significant narrative. It's a segment often overlooked, overshadowed by the glitz and glamour of the grandstand. But the bustling concession stands, where the aromas of hotdogs and popcorn mingle in the air, embody a unique cadence within the economic harmony. Patrons stand in line, not merely seeking sustenance, but an immersion in the fullness of the experience. The delectable offerings—those steaming hotdogs, the fragrant popcorn, the array of beverages—extend beyond the realm of gastronomy. They become part of the ritual, a cherished routine that transcends appetite. It's a shared experience that the fans savor, a sensory expression of their engagement. Through the shared act of indulging in these culinary delights, they are, in essence, partaking in a ritual that solidifies their connection to the game, enhancing the collective atmosphere of camaraderie and celebration.

## Annual League Revenue·

| NFL | NBA | NHL |
|-----|-----|-----|
| $17.19 B | $6.41 B | $5.3 B |

| MLB | MLS |
|-----|-----|
| $9.56 B | $1 B |

*2025. Source: Statista.com

## NFL Broadcasting Revenue

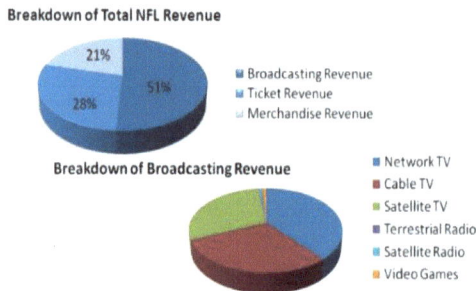

**Breakdown of Total NFL Revenue**

- 21%
- 51%
- 28%

■ Broadcasting Revenue
■ Ticket Revenue
□ Merchandise Revenue

**Breakdown of Broadcasting Revenue**

■ Network TV
■ Cable TV
■ Satellite TV
■ Terrestrial Radio
■ Satellite Radio
■ Video Games

•Broadcasting revenue generated by television provides the most revenue for the NFL and given that there is substantially less international demand, it can be assumed that international broadcasting generates a smaller portion of overall revenue.
•By not focusing on the dollar amount of broadcasting revenue generated internationally in the short term, could trying a "push" strategy, where international TV networks or satellite stations carry all regular season games, have the potential to generate additional interest in the NFL abroad, thereby helping the NFL in the long term?

Moreover, the 21st century has heralded a new layer to this symphony—the rise of digital engagement. Smartphones and tablets have become extensions of fandom, and the NFL has capitalized on this trend to craft intricate digital platforms that facilitate interaction. In this virtual arena, fantasy leagues, mobile apps, and social media hubs converge to create a tapestry of connectivity. Fans don't just spectate; they actively engage, discuss, and share their experience in real time, amplifying the resonance of the game beyond the confines of the stadium. This digital camaraderie, while intangible, marks the advent of a new age of fan engagement. It transcends the limitations of geography, traverses time zones, and forms a new conduit through which the game's aura can be experienced.

In the ultimate synthesis, the economics of game day transcend the mere confines of the field. They blossom into an intricate ballet—a choreography of revenue streams that encapsulate the convergence of sports and commerce. The symphony resonates through ticket sales, media rights, merchandise, culinary indulgence, and digital connectivity, all coalescing into a grand tableau. It's a harmony that harmonizes the fervor of the fans with the pragmatism of business, melding passion and profit, excitement and enterprise. As the stadium lights blaze and the referee's whistle pierces the air, this symphony crescendos, capturing the essence of a timeless truth—the fusion of sports and economics, an eternal bond woven seamlessly into the fabric of modern society.

**The Business behind Super Bowl LIV**

SPORTS BUSINESS INSTITUTE BARCELONA

**$6,390**
Average ticket price

**149 Million**
Total TV audience of Super Bowl in 2019

**2 Million**
Estimated number of pizzas sold by Domino's

**$5.6 Million**
Average cost of a 30-second advert during game

**$860,000**
Salary of an average NFL player with over 3 years in NFL

**$6.8 billion**
Amount of money set to be gambled for Super Bowl LIV

Data obtained from:
Forbes
CNBC
Sports Illustrated
NFL
Domino's

**$124,000**
Total bonuses per player for winning side

🐦📷 @sbi_Barcelona    www.sbibarcelona.com    f SportsBusinessInstituteBarcelona

# New Releases

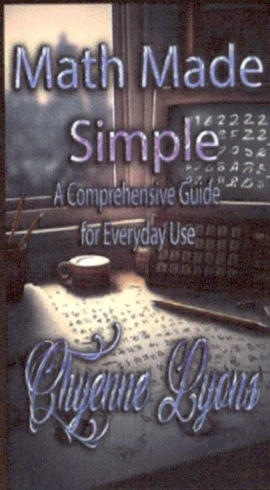

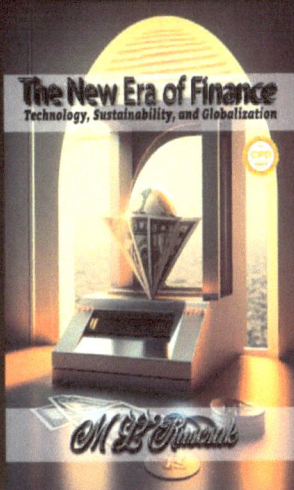

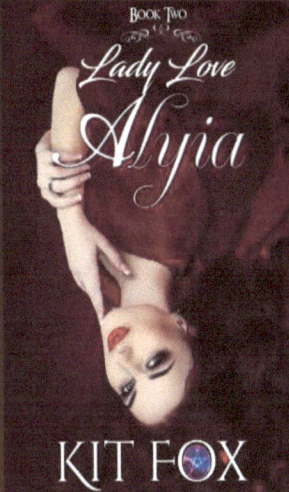

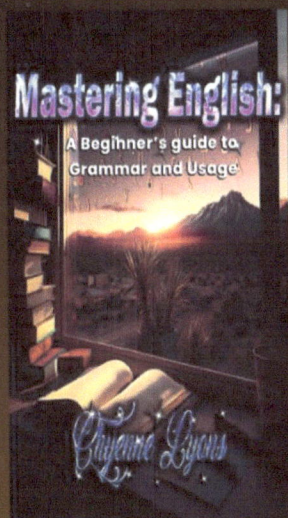

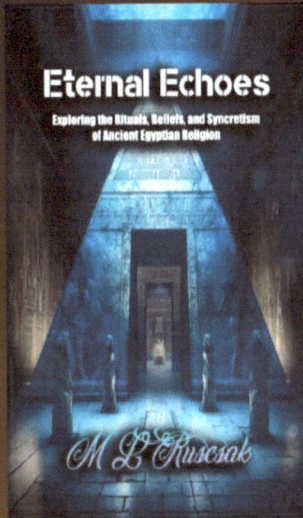

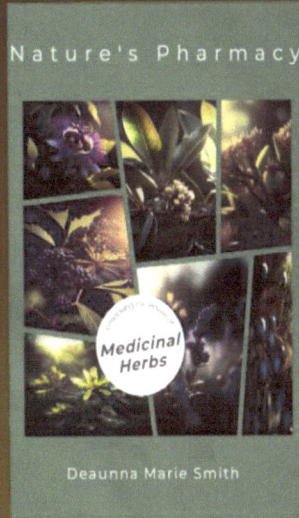

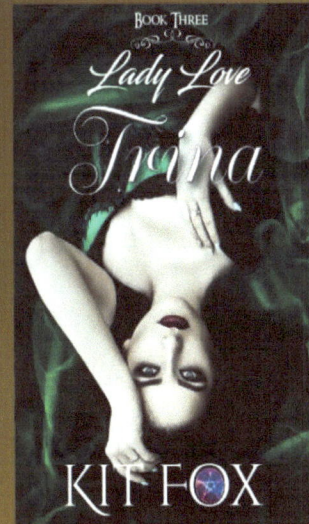

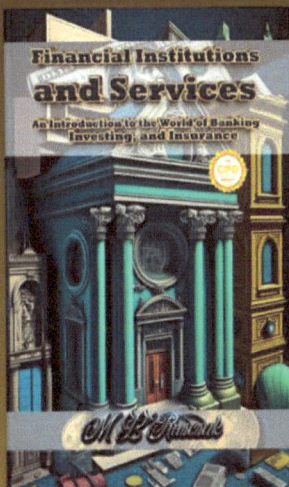

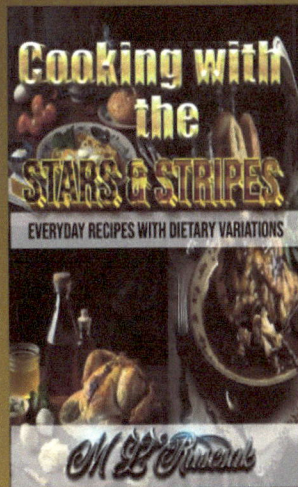

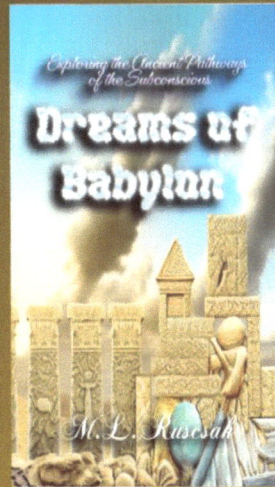

# ENTREPRENEUR TIPS AND TRICKS

## Crossing the Goal Line: NFL-Inspired Entrepreneur Tips for Crossover Success

- **Strategize Like a Coach:** Just as NFL coaches craft intricate game plans, entrepreneurs should develop strategic roadmaps. Plan for short-term wins while keeping the long game in sight.

- **Build a Winning Team:** Like NFL teams seek diverse talents, assemble a team with varied skills. Collaborative strengths ensure your business can tackle any challenge.

- **Adapt to Changing Defenses:** In business, market dynamics shift. Stay agile, adapt your playbook, and pivot when needed to remain competitive in ever-changing landscapes.

- **Leverage the Power of Branding:** The NFL's iconic teams show the power of branding. Develop a strong brand identity that resonates with your audience and becomes synonymous with excellence.

- **Embrace Calculated Risks:** NFL plays involve calculated risks. Similarly, entrepreneurs should take informed chances, weighing potential rewards against potential setbacks.

- **Master the Art of Negotiation:** Negotiations are a cornerstone of both NFL deals and business agreements. Develop strong negotiation skills to secure beneficial partnerships.

- **Fan Engagement Is Key:** Just as fans fuel the NFL's success, customers are crucial to business growth. Engage your audience through personalized experiences and effective communication.

- **Harness Digital Technologies:** Like the NFL's embrace of technology, leverage digital tools to streamline operations, enhance customer interactions, and stay ahead of the curve.

- **Innovate Like a Play Designer:** NFL teams create innovative plays. Entrepreneurs, too, should consistently innovate to offer unique products or services that stand out in the market.

- **Resilience in the Face of Adversity:** NFL players overcome setbacks. As an entrepreneur, build resilience to navigate challenges, learning from failures and rebounding stronger.

JUST AS NFL STRATEGIES CAN BE TRANSLATED INTO BUSINESS ACUMEN, THESE TIPS OFFER A PLAYBOOK FOR ENTREPRENEURS TO ACHIEVE CROSSOVER SUCCESS.

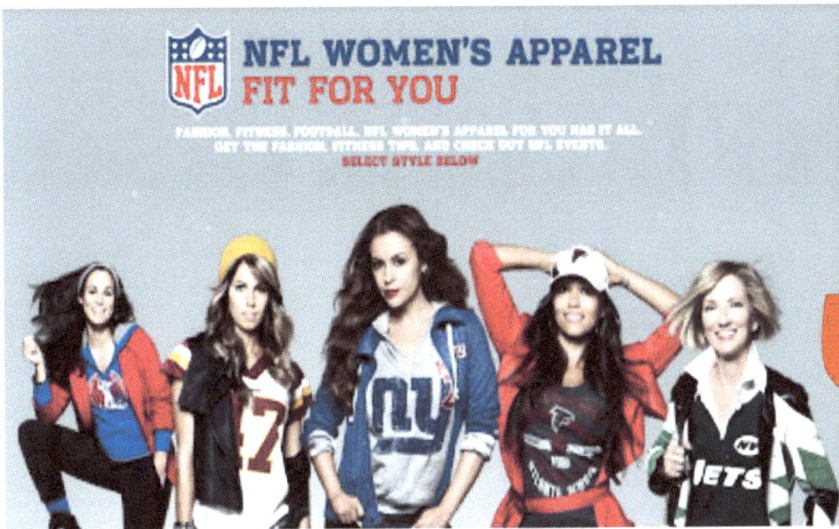

**NFL WOMEN'S APPAREL FIT FOR YOU**

FASHION, FITNESS, FOOTBALL, NFL WOMEN'S APPAREL FOR YOU HAS IT ALL.
GET THE FASHION, FITNESS TIPS, AND CHECK OUT NFL EVENTS.
SELECT STYLE BELOW

# BUILDING A WINNING BRAND:
## MARKETING STRATEGIES FROM NFL TEAMS

**NEWS PROVIDED BY: TRIENT PRESS**

Building a Winning Brand: Unveiling Marketing Strategies from the Playbook of NFL Teams

In the modern arena of sport and business, where the lines between athletic prowess and marketing acumen converge, a symphony of strategies emerges, as NFL teams showcase not only their prowess on the field but also their mastery in building winning brands. Behind the fervor of touchdowns and tackles lies a sophisticated playbook of marketing strategies that transcend the realm of sport, offering invaluable lessons to businesses seeking to elevate their brand game.

### 1. The Power of Storytelling: Crafting a Narrative Beyond the Game

The NFL has perfected the art of storytelling, weaving compelling narratives around teams, players, and rivalries. This storytelling transcends the game, forming a narrative that resonates with fans on an emotional level. Brands, too, can benefit from weaving captivating stories that evoke emotions, engage audiences, and create lasting connections. By embracing a narrative that goes beyond the transactional, brands can foster deeper relationships with their customers.

### 2. Cultivating a Strong Visual Identity: The Iconic Uniforms and Logos

The visual identity of NFL teams is etched into the hearts of millions. From the iconic Dallas Cowboys star to the green and gold of the Green Bay Packers, each team's colors and logos become symbols of loyalty and identity. Businesses should emulate this by creating a distinct visual identity that aligns with their brand values and leaves an indelible mark in the minds of consumers. A strong visual identity enhances brand recognition and ensures consistency across all touchpoints.

### 3. Engaging the Community: Beyond the Stadium

NFL teams don't just exist within the confines of the stadium; they extend their reach into local communities. Whether through community service, charity partnerships, or youth programs, NFL teams establish themselves as integral parts of their communities. Businesses can follow suit by engaging in corporate social responsibility initiatives that resonate with their target audience and contribute to social betterment. This community engagement not only enhances brand reputation but also fosters a sense of purpose.

### 4. Leveraging Influencer Partnerships: The Player-Brand Connection

Endorsement deals between NFL players and brands showcase the symbiotic relationship between athleticism and business. These partnerships leverage player influence to expand brand reach. Businesses should seek partnerships that align with their values and resonate with their audience, capitalizing on the credibility and reach of influencers. This influencer collaboration adds authenticity to brand messaging and extends its reach to new demographics.

### 5. Creating Memorable Experiences: Game Day and Beyond

Game day experiences transcend the final score, becoming immersive journeys for fans. From tailgating to halftime shows, the NFL crafts experiences that stick in the minds of attendees. Businesses can learn from this by creating memorable customer experiences that extend beyond transactions, fostering loyalty and advocacy. Whether through in-store events, personalized interactions, or interactive content, brands can create moments that resonate long after the initial interaction.

In the arena where the NFL's marketing prowess shines, businesses can uncover a treasure trove of strategies to build winning brands. By taking cues from the NFL playbook, brands can forge deeper connections, evoke emotions, and carve their names in the annals of consumer consciousness. Just as NFL teams are more than players on the field, brands, too, can transcend their products, becoming part of a larger narrative that resonates with audiences far beyond the transaction. As the NFL demonstrates, building a winning brand is a strategic symphony, where each note contributes to the harmonious crescendo of lasting success.

# THE POWER OF FANDOM:
## How NFL Teams
### CULTIVATE LOYAL CUSTOMER BASES

## Marketing

In the heart-pounding realm where sport and business intersect, a phenomenon of unparalleled loyalty and fervor takes center stage. Behind the grandeur of touchdowns and tackles lies a potent lesson in customer engagement that businesses, irrespective of industry, can learn from–the resounding power of fandom, as exemplified by the masterful orchestration of NFL teams. Beyond mere games, these teams nurture and cultivate a tribe of unwavering supporters, showcasing a strategic symphony that harmonizes the values of athletic pursuit with the shrewd principles of brand loyalty.

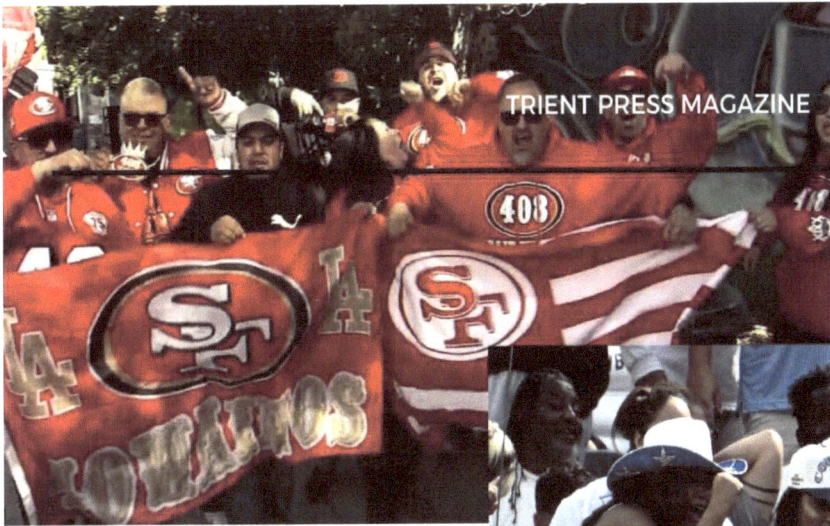

## The Genesis of Connection: Fandom as Identity:

NFL teams have honed the art of transforming ordinary individuals into fervent fans who identify with the team's ethos. This transformation goes beyond the superficial; it's an integration of values, aspirations, and a sense of belonging. Businesses can emulate this by fostering connections with their customer base, resonating with shared values and aspirations. When customers see their identity reflected in a brand, a powerful bond forms.

## The Ritual of Gameday: Emotion-Fueled Engagement

Game day is more than a mere contest—it's a ritualistic experience that fuels emotions and forges memories. NFL teams masterfully curate these experiences, drawing fans into a narrative that extends beyond the game itself. Businesses can tap into this by creating engaging experiences that evoke emotions and resonate with their audience. Whether through special events, limited-time offers, or immersive interactions, businesses can emulate the ritualistic fervor that game day evokes.

## The Art of Brand Storytelling: Transcending the Field

NFL teams spin intricate narratives that weave players, history, and rivalries into captivating tales. These stories transcend the field, resonating deeply with fans and embedding the team within their lives. Businesses can leverage this by crafting compelling brand stories that capture the essence of their journey. A well-crafted narrative can transform a brand from a transactional entity to a cherished part of customers' stories.

## Nurturing a Community: Shared Passion as Glue

NFL teams create vibrant communities that extend beyond geographic boundaries. Fans find camaraderie among fellow supporters, united by shared passion. Businesses should strive to create similar communities, fostering a sense of belonging among customers. This sense of community not only enhances loyalty but also provides a platform for customers to advocate for the brand.

## Accessibility and Inclusivity: Expanding the Fold

NFL teams engage fans through various touchpoints, from social media to stadium events. This accessibility cultivates inclusivity, ensuring that fans from all walks of life feel part of the tribe. Businesses can learn from this approach by creating multiple avenues for engagement and ensuring that every customer feels valued and included.

In the captivating world where the NFL reigns supreme, businesses are privy to a masterclass in customer loyalty. The power of fandom, the art of engagement, and the mastery of storytelling—the NFL's playbook holds vital insights for any enterprise seeking to create an unwavering customer base. Beyond the realm of sport, the symphony of loyalty resounds as a universal truth—when businesses nurture the power of fandom, they orchestrate a harmonious bond that transcends transactions, fostering lasting loyalty that echoes through time.

Beyond Sponsorships:

# Exploring Multifaceted NFL-Brand Collaborations

In the realm where sports and business intersect, a new breed of partnerships has emerged that transcends conventional sponsorships. Multifaceted NFL-brand collaborations are redefining the landscape of modern marketing, forging connections that go beyond logos on jerseys to delve deep into meaningful interactions, captivating narratives, and shared values. This article delves into this thriving territory, uncovering how the NFL and brands are crafting collaborations that resonate profoundly with fans and consumers alike.

Modern collaborations between the NFL and brands have moved beyond traditional sponsorships, aiming to elevate the fan experience to unprecedented heights. No longer confined to mere brand visibility during game time, these partnerships create interactive fan zones, immersive pre-game activations, and exclusive events that enrich the fan journey. By extending engagement beyond the stadium, brands create excitement that resonates beyond the final whistle.

In the pursuit of innovation, the NFL and brands are aligning their technological advances to create compelling partnerships. From leveraging cutting-edge technology to enhance viewer experience to integrating smart devices for a seamlessly connected game day, these collaborations tap into the shared drive to push boundaries. These partnerships position brands as enablers of innovation, appealing to tech-savvy consumers seeking the integration of sports and lifestyle.

*Melisa Ruscsak*
Editor-in-Chief

*Trient Press Magazine*

NFL EDITION 2023

Multifaceted NFL-brand collaborations are grounded in crafting narratives that intertwine with the essence of the game. Brands leverage the league's history, players, and cultural impact to create stories that resonate with fans. These narratives extend beyond commercials, creating a continuum of storytelling that bridges the brand's identity with the spirit of football itself. By aligning with the emotional core of the sport, brands forge connections that endure.

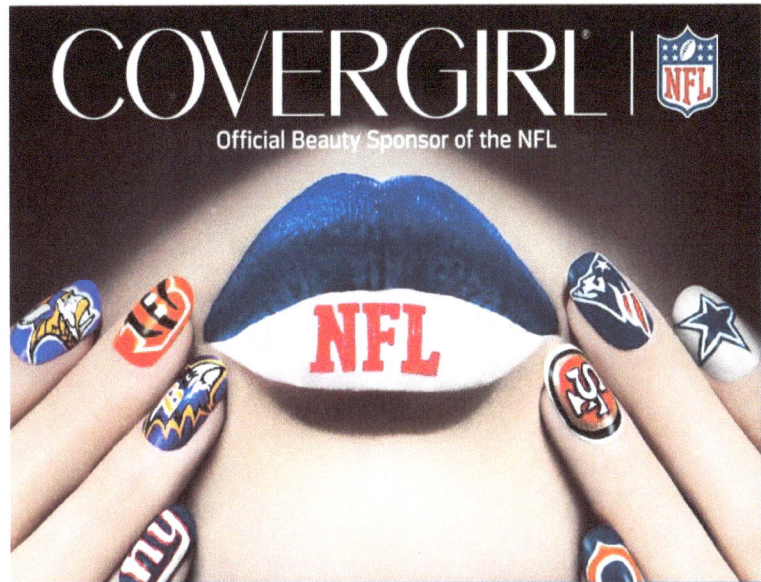

"Within the tapestry of multifaceted NFL-brand collaborations, narratives are woven that transcend commerce and resonate with the heart of the game. Brands harness the league's legacy, its players, and the cultural reverberations to craft stories that find a home in fans' hearts. These stories, extending beyond the confines of advertisements, create an unbroken thread of storytelling that unites the brand's essence with the very soul of football. Through this alignment with the sport's emotional resonance, brands build connections that stand the test of time."

### Elevating Collaborations: Brands as Agents of Societal Change

Yet, these collaborations transcend the realm of marketing objectives, opening doors to impactful change on a broader scale. Brands seize the opportunity to align with the NFL's initiatives for social justice, utilizing their influential platforms to amplify vital messages of equality, unity, and positive transformation. In taking up this mantle, these collaborations represent a paradigm shift towards purpose-driven marketing—a landscape where brands metamorphose into fervent advocates for causes that deeply resonate with fans and consumers. This alignment with the forward march of societal progress infuses the brand narrative with purpose and strikes a resounding chord with a conscious consumer base.

## The Authentic Tapestry: Weaving Brands into the Fan Experience

At the heart of multifaceted NFL-brand collaborations lies an indispensable thread—authenticity. This intricate weaving of brands into the fan experience is a testament to the core of these partnerships. Seamlessly integrated, brands become an integral part of the game's fabric, enhancing the fan journey without breaching its sanctity. This fusion of authenticity not only engenders trust but also bolsters brand credibility. Brands, now organically interwoven into the fan's journey, fortify relationships and etch themselves as genuine companions on this immersive adventure. In a world cluttered with marketing messages, authenticity emerges as the golden currency of connection.

## Unite with Authentic Fan Experiences!

## The Bold Redefinition: Collaborations as Dynamic Ventures

The dynamic universe of marketing witnesses a seismic redefinition through multifaceted NFL-brand collaborations. These transcendent partnerships stretch the boundaries of conventional sponsorships, curating experiences that go beyond passive transactions. They craft immersive stories that resonate, champion social causes that matter, and seamlessly embed brands within the very essence of the sport. In doing so, they echo a profound lesson: the future of collaboration hinges on the synergy of shared values, innovative thinking, and a relentless commitment to amplifying the fan experience.

As marketers navigate this uncharted terrain, a clear revelation emerges—the true essence of partnerships thrives in the harmonious symphony between the NFL and brands. It's a symphony where commerce dances with passion, innovation meets authenticity, and stories merge with shared values. These resonant partnerships ripple beyond mere transactions, touching the hearts of fans and consumers alike, affirming that the power of collaboration is not in its endpoint, but in the symphonic journey it embarks upon.

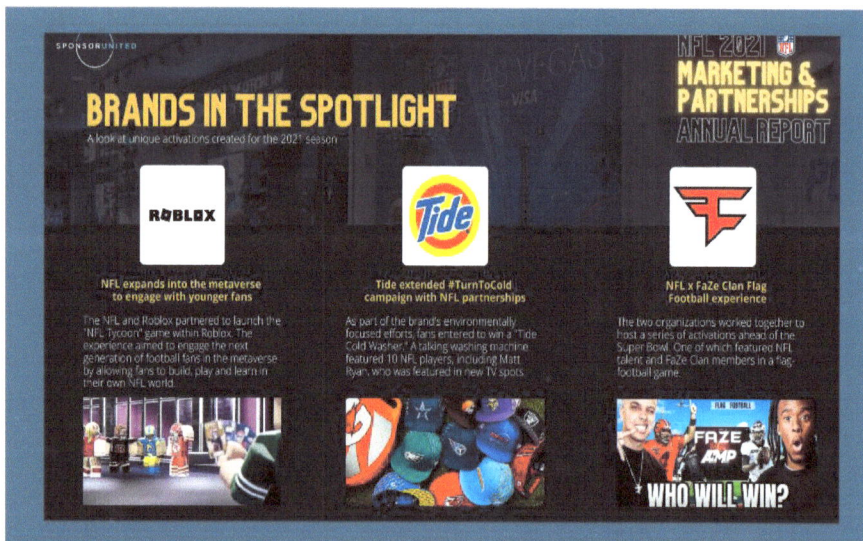

BRANDS IN THE SPOTLIGHT
A look at unique activations created for the 2021 season

NFL 2021
MARKETING & PARTNERSHIPS
ANNUAL REPORT

ROBLOX — NFL expands into the metaverse to engage with younger fans

Tide — Tide extended #TurnToCold campaign with NFL partnerships

FaZe — NFL x FaZe Clan Flag Football experience

# Trientrepreneur

A Trient Press Publication for Authors & Entrepreneurs

*Spring into Suc...*

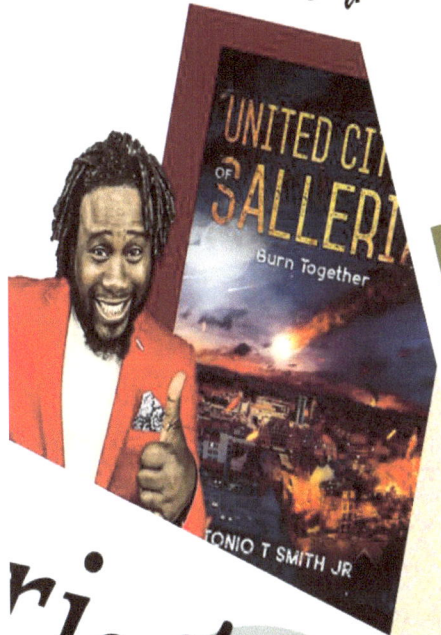

UNITED CITY OF SALLERI

Burn Together

TONIO T SMITH JR

# Trientrepreneur

A Trient Press Publication for Authors & Entrepreneurs

*Unleash Your Business Potential*

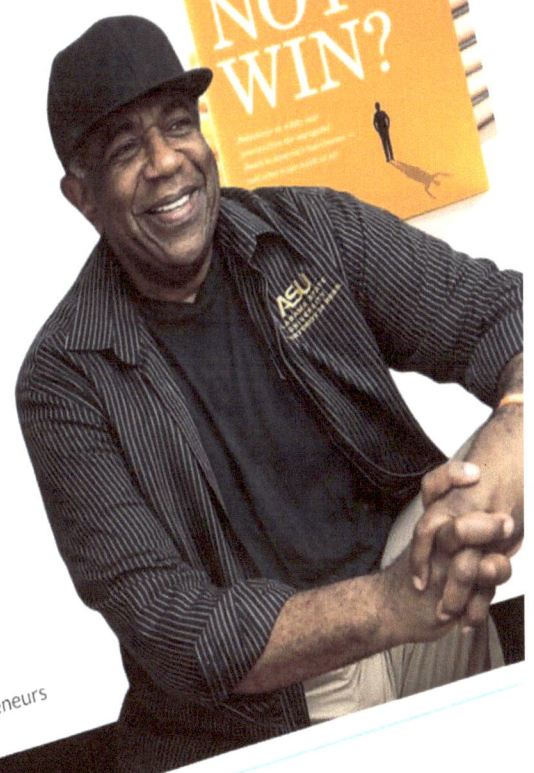

Issue 13 | August/ September 2023

## FEATURED

LARRY D. THORNTON:
AUTHOR, KEYNOTE
SPEAKER, AND CEO

Unleashing Your Creative Potential

## ARTICLES

AI in Everyday Use:
Transforming How We Live
Interact in the Digital
Age

...g the
...olution

...ING WITH
...RIENT
...S FOR FINDING
INSPIRATION IN
TRAVEL

## TIPS

Resources for Entrepreneurs
and Authors

LARRY D. THORNTON

WHY NOT WIN?

# Trientrepreneur

A Trient Press Publication for Authors & Entrepreneurs

# TRIENTREPRENEUR
# MAGAZINE
## WHAT'S IN YOUR TOOL BOX

Embark on a journey of wisdom and camaraderie at Dove and Dragon Radio. Tune in for riveting conversations spanning business strategies, travel tales, and more.

## THE WORLD EVOLVES, RADIO TRANSFORMS.

### WELCOME TO A NEW ERA OF AUDITORY EXPLORATION.

DOVE AND DRAGON

RADIO

# Gridiron Success Stories
## How NFL Players Tackle Entrepreneurship

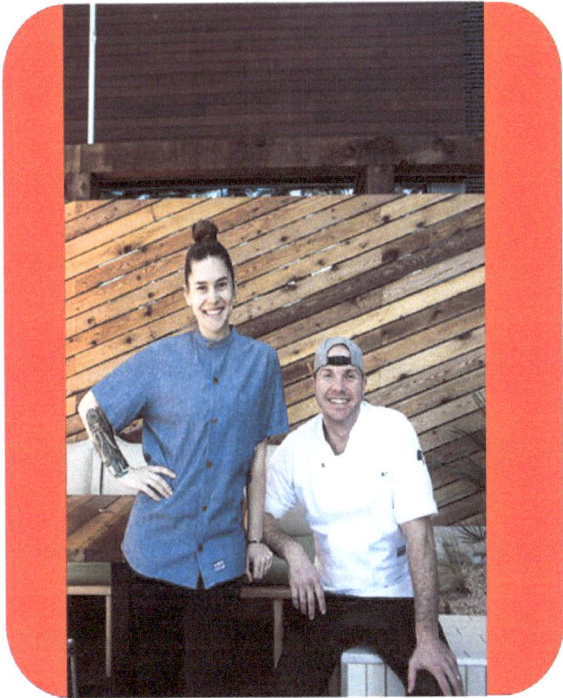

Within the illustrious realm of professional football, where the gridiron stands as an arena for showcasing unparalleled athletic prowess, a parallel game unfolds—one of entrepreneurial acumen. As NFL players make the transition from the frenetic field of tackles and touchdowns to the dynamic landscape of business, they demonstrate that the very same drive and determination that propelled them to triumph on the athletic stage can be seamlessly channeled into the realm of entrepreneurship. With each step they take off the field, they venture into uncharted territories, from venture capital to startups, carrying with them a winning mindset that knows no boundaries. This article is a journey into the captivating narratives of these NFL players who have not merely transitioned but have risen to conquer the challenges of entrepreneurship with the same unwavering fervor that marked their celebrated athletic careers. By delving into their stories, we uncover a playbook teeming with insights, strategies, and principles that lay the foundation for achieving resounding success in the dynamic world of business. In essence, this exploration unveils a bridge connecting the pursuit of victory on the field to the pursuit of triumph in the entrepreneurial sphere, showcasing that the relentless pursuit of excellence is a universal trait that knows no boundaries.

## The Crossroads of Ambition: Transitioning from End Zones to Boardrooms

The transition from the vibrant arenas of professional football to the unfurling possibilities of the business world marks a pivotal crossroads for NFL players. As they bid adieu to the exhilaration of end zones and touchdowns, they find themselves at an intersection where ambition converges with a palpable sense of uncertainty. However, this juncture isn't merely a moment of reflection—it's a canvas upon which a new narrative is drawn. In the face of uncertainty, a distinct group of players have stepped forth, not with trepidation, but with a vision that propels them forward.

These athletes, fortified with the discipline, determination, and an indomitable work ethic that has been meticulously honed on the field, embark on a journey that traverses from familiar turf to uncharted territories—the realm of entrepreneurship. This journey is marked by strategic vision that weaves their athletic prowess into the fabric of business innovation. With a playbook that encompasses leadership acumen, the art of teamwork, and the resilience to overcome adversities, they boldly venture into the world of startups and ventures.

COMING SOON

3443 Laguna Blvd
Inside the Elk Grove
Sports Center
Elk Grove, CA 95750

DOUBLE ★ NICKEL
55
SMOKEHOUSE
SmokeHouse55.com

09.01.14

55

Their transition is not one of mere replication, but of transformation. As they shift from the rigors of sports to the intricacies of business, they channel their competitive spirit into a new arena. The fervor that once fueled touchdowns and tackles is now seamlessly interwoven with strategic thinking and calculated risk-taking. This infusion of spirit enables them to tackle the challenges of entrepreneurship with a fervor akin to their athletic pursuits, proving that the drive for excellence isn't confined to the gridiron—it's a force that fuels their pursuit of success in any arena.

As these players venture into the boardrooms with a playbook that extends beyond the tangible field, they bring with them an inherent understanding of leadership dynamics and the value of collaboration. Just as they orchestrated plays and strategies on the field, they now employ their innate ability to lead, to guide, and to adapt. This synergy between their sporting legacy and their entrepreneurial endeavors creates a harmonious symphony that echoes across their ventures.

In the world of entrepreneurship, these players do not merely dwell on the laurels of their past accomplishments; they write a new chapter, infusing their businesses with the very essence that defined their careers—passion, perseverance, and a relentless pursuit of victory. The crossroads of ambition become the threshold to transformation, reminding us that the transition from end zones to boardrooms isn't a concession, but an evolution—an evolution marked by an unwavering commitment to excellence, regardless of the arena.

## REDEFINING VICTORY: UNVEILING THE ENTREPRENEURIAL SCOREBOARD

When NFL players transition from the electrifying theater of the gridiron to the intricate arena of entrepreneurship, they embark on a transformative journey that reshapes the very metrics of success. No longer confined to the traditional yardsticks of touchdowns and tackles, this new frontier introduces a dynamic recalibration of success—a recalibration that embraces multifaceted dimensions and resonates far beyond the boundaries of the playing field.

As these players venture into the entrepreneurial realm, the scoreboard of achievement undergoes a profound metamorphosis. The once linear measure of touchdowns is now augmented by a tapestry of multifarious indicators: revenue growth, market share expansion, and the litmus test of customer satisfaction. This composite scoreboard is a testament to the nuanced landscape they now navigate, where success transcends mere athletic achievements and extends into the realm of strategic vision and business acumen.

Harnessing the momentum of their personal brands and networks—forged through years of rigorous training, heart-pounding victories, and fervent fan following—these players wield their status as NFL luminaries as a potent catalyst. Their ascent from the pinnacle of athletic glory to the realm of entrepreneurship isn't merely a pivot; it's a testament to the kaleidoscope of their skills. It underscores their innate ability to adapt, innovate, and excel,

transcending the boundaries of their sports careers to become architects of success in the world of business.

As these players translate their on-field stardom into business ventures, they harness the power of their personas to spotlight their enterprises. The spotlight of the stadium yields to the spotlight of the market, and their businesses are propelled to the forefront. This spotlight isn't transient; it's a consequence of their dedication, their mastery, and their unparalleled influence. This transition symbolizes the fusion of two realms—athletic prowess and entrepreneurial insight—that epitomizes the holistic versatility of their capabilities.

In essence, the journey from athlete to entrepreneur is an ode to the expansiveness of human potential. It's a symphony that harmonizes dedication with diversification, athletic triumphs with business victories, and personal branding with market positioning. The entrepreneurial scoreboard, painted with hues of growth, influence, and strategic accomplishment, reflects their legacy—an unceasing pursuit of excellence that transcends the conventional and ushers in an era where success is defined not by a single metric, but by the harmonious orchestration of myriad achievements.

## THE HUDDLE OF MENTORSHIP: NAVIGATING THE TRANSITION WITH GUIDING LIGHTS

As NFL players make the leap from the stadium to the boardroom, a resounding truth emerges—the journey from athlete to entrepreneur is paved with challenges, complexities, and uncertainties. In this intricate labyrinth of business creation, a vital element rises as a guiding light, providing a compass for these individuals as they navigate the uncharted waters of entrepreneurship. This guiding light is none other than mentorship—an indispensable force that bridges the gap between the familiar realm of the field and the unexplored landscape of business.

The stories of NFL players-turned-entrepreneurs are not just tales of athletic prowess, but narratives of versatility and adaptability. This transition isn't merely a change of scenery; it's a transformation of identity. As these players recalibrate their roles from being warriors of the gridiron to becoming architects of business ventures, they enter a realm that demands a different skill set, a fresh perspective, and a strategic mindset. In this juncture of transformation, mentorship emerges as the cornerstone upon which their entrepreneurial journey rests.

Enter seasoned entrepreneurs and accomplished business leaders—individuals who have navigated the complexities of the business world and have emerged victorious. These mentors take on the role of guiding lights, offering insights that are worth their weight in gold. From lessons learned in the trenches to strategic maneuvers executed with precision, these mentors share a tapestry of experiences that form the foundation for player-entrepreneurs to build upon. Their guidance serves as a roadmap, illuminating potential pitfalls and charting pathways to seize opportunities.

The huddle of mentorship is akin to a well-choreographed symphony. It provides play-by-play guidance, ensuring that the player-entrepreneurs are equipped with the knowledge and foresight needed to make informed decisions. The mentors act as quarterbacks of advice, calling out the plays that maximize the chances of success while minimizing the risks. This guidance isn't theoretical—it's grounded in real-world experiences, providing practical insights that serve as a compass in the often turbulent waters of entrepreneurship.

However, the mentorship journey isn't solely about pragmatic guidance; it's a holistic experience that encompasses emotional support and personal growth. These mentors become pillars of strength, offering reassurance during moments of doubt and instilling confidence in the player-entrepreneurs' abilities. They provide a safe space for questions, a platform for discussions, and a source of motivation that propels these individuals to reach their fullest potential.

The transition from athlete to entrepreneur is not a solitary endeavor; it's a collaborative odyssey marked by the resonance of teamwork. Just as the huddle on the football field unites players to strategize and execute plays, the huddle of mentorship unites player-entrepreneurs with mentors who are invested in their success. This collaborative ethos is a reflection of the values ingrained in their NFL careers—the understanding that victory is a collective endeavor.

In essence, the huddle of mentorship symbolizes the harmony between tradition and evolution. It honors the legacy of NFL players while embracing their evolution into a new arena. Through mentorship, these player-entrepreneurs find the guidance, support, and wisdom needed to bridge the gap between the gridiron and the business world. The journey is no longer a solo expedition—it's a collaborative symphony of shared insights, collective wisdom, and a relentless pursuit of excellence that underscores the undeniable truth: just as a football team is greater than the sum of its parts, so too is the journey from the field to the realm of entrepreneurship fortified by the power of mentorship.

JOHN ELWAY

DEALERSHIP GROUP

## THE HUDDLE OF MENTORSHIP: NAVIGATING ENTREPRENEURSHIP'S PATH WITH GUIDING LIGHTS

For those NFL players who have transitioned from the intensity of the field to the intricacies of entrepreneurship, the journey is illuminated by a guiding light—mentorship. In this new arena, seasoned entrepreneurs and astute business leaders step into the role of mentors, offering a steady hand and invaluable insights that help these athletes navigate the uncharted waters of business creation. This huddle of mentorship emerges as a critical component, providing strategic direction, emotional support, and a treasure trove of practical knowledge.

The transition from the adrenaline-charged environment of professional sports to the strategic landscape of business is not a solitary endeavor; it's a symphony conducted with the wisdom of those who have tread similar paths. The mentorship network becomes a sanctuary of shared experiences and hard-earned lessons, a space where questions find answers, challenges find solutions, and uncertainty finds clarity.

In this mentorship huddle, a play-by-play approach is embraced. Much like an NFL coach calling out plays in real-time, mentors provide guidance that is both timely and precise. Pitfalls are anticipated and circumvented, opportunities are seized with calculated precision, and strategies are formulated with an astute understanding of the evolving business landscape. This play-by-play mentorship isn't a one-size-fits-all approach; it's a dynamic exchange that adapts to the nuances of each player-entrepreneur's journey.

Crucially, the mentorship journey is not merely about avoiding mistakes; it's about fostering growth. Just as athletes evolve through training and practice, these player-entrepreneurs grow under the wings of their mentors. This process of growth, driven by the collective wisdom of mentors, empowers these individuals to make informed decisions, forge strategic alliances, and navigate complexities with a heightened acumen that transcends what could be achieved individually.

This mentorship journey isn't just a mirroring of the teamwork ingrained in their NFL careers; it's an elevation of that very principle. Just as a football team rallies together to achieve victory, the mentorship huddle for player-entrepreneurs becomes a collective effort to achieve business success. This collaboration is emblematic of the ethos that fuels their NFL careers—teamwork, unity, and the collective pursuit of a shared goal.

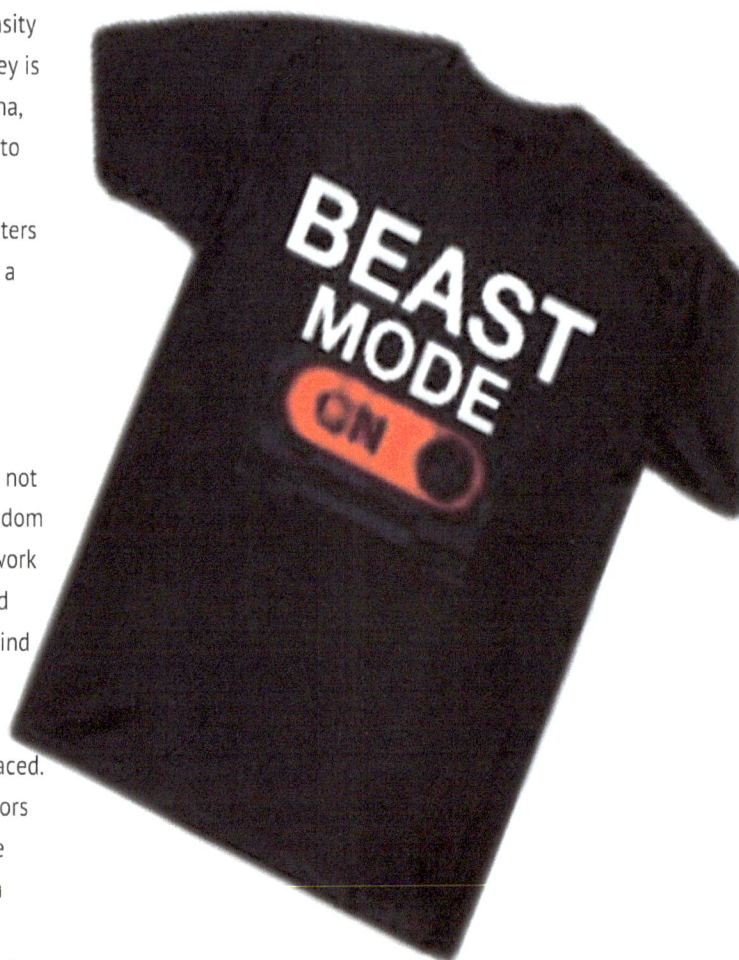

As they transition from the familiar confines of the field to the ever-shifting terrain of entrepreneurship, these players-turned-entrepreneurs embrace the mentorship journey with humility and eagerness. It's a journey that embodies the essence of continuous learning, adaptation, and growth. In the huddle of mentorship, they find more than just guidance; they find a transformative experience that encapsulates the spirit of collaboration, underscoring that success isn't merely an individual pursuit—it's a collective symphony orchestrated with the guidance of mentors who illuminate the path to triumph.

## FROM ATHLETE TO VISIONARY: SHAPING LEGACIES BEYOND THE FIELD

The journey from the realm of professional sports to the horizon of entrepreneurship is a testament to the boundless capacity of human potential. The transition isn't merely a shift in career—it's a deliberate choice to redefine one's legacy. For those who have etched their names in the annals of athletic history, this transition is not an endpoint; rather, it's a new chapter, one marked by the evolution from athlete to visionary.

The narrative of these individuals is a profound testament to versatility, adaptability, and the unwavering commitment to excellence that defines their core. The accolades amassed on the field become the foundation upon which they build new dreams, new goals, and new realms of impact. As they pivot from their role as athletes to the role of visionaries, they embark on a journey that challenges conventional narratives, defies expectations, and leaves an indelible mark on the world of business.

In many ways, the journey from athlete to visionary mirrors the essence of entrepreneurship itself—an audacious leap into the unknown, driven by the pursuit of innovation, the willingness to take calculated risks, and the unrelenting desire to reshape the status quo. Just as they once stepped onto the field with a determination to conquer opponents, these individuals step into the world of business with the determination to conquer challenges and seize opportunities.

The transition isn't marked by the relinquishment of one identity for another; it's an integration of both. The leadership skills, the resilience to overcome adversities, and the ability to perform under pressure—qualities honed on the field—become invaluable assets in the realm of entrepreneurship. Just as a quarterback orchestrates plays, these visionaries orchestrate strategies, leveraging their innate ability to lead, inspire, and adapt.

The legacy they once crafted through touchdowns and tackles is now extended through innovative ideas, groundbreaking ventures, and a commitment to create lasting change. The field of play may have shifted, but the pursuit of excellence remains steadfast. The metrics of success transform from yards gained to markets conquered, from points scored to lives impacted. This transformation isn't just a personal endeavor; it's a resonance of the transformative power of human potential.

From athlete to visionary, this journey encapsulates the essence of evolution. It's a manifestation of the unyielding spirit to transcend limitations, to break barriers, and to redefine what's possible. The transition doesn't erase their athletic legacy—it enriches it. The stories they tell are no longer confined to the realm of sports; they're narratives of transformation, of innovation, and of creating legacies that extend far beyond the boundaries of the field.

In the end, the journey from athlete to visionary is a testament to the infinite capacity to redefine oneself, to shape new horizons, and to leave an indelible mark on the world. As they trade in their jerseys for tailored suits, their cleats for the boardroom, they enter a realm where success isn't measured by victories alone, but by the lasting impact they create. It's a journey that illuminates the path of human potential, and in doing so, they redefine not just their legacies, but the very essence of what it means to be a visionary.

## THE ENTREPRENEUR'S ARENA: UNVEILING LESSONS FOR ASPIRING BUSINESS LEADERS

The transition from the stadium to the world of business is a symphony of transformation—one that holds invaluable lessons for those aspiring to lead in the realms of entrepreneurship. The journeys embarked upon by NFL players-turned-entrepreneurs are a treasure trove of insights, offering a lens through which we can decipher the blueprint of success in the dynamic landscape of business.

These stories resonate as a reminder of the boundless potential of skills transfer. The traits that propelled these individuals to achieve athletic greatness find resonance in their entrepreneurial pursuits. The determination that fueled their pursuit of touchdowns now ignites their quest for innovation and market domination. This seamless transfer of skills underscores the cross-disciplinary nature of success—an endeavor where the spirit of excellence knows no boundaries.

In the arena of entrepreneurship, the role of continuous learning becomes paramount. NFL players who venture into this landscape embrace the ethos of constant evolution. They recognize that success isn't a static destination; it's an ongoing journey fueled by a hunger for knowledge. Just as they studied playbooks and analyzed opponents, they immerse themselves in the world of market trends, customer dynamics, and emerging technologies. This appetite for knowledge becomes a hallmark of their entrepreneurial journey.

daptation is a cornerstone in both the world of sports and the world of business. The ability to pivot strategies in response to changing dynamics is a shared trait that these players-turned-entrepreneurs possess. Just as they adjusted their game plans based on the opponent's tactics, they recalibrate their business strategies based on market shifts and consumer demands. This flexibility resonates as a powerful lesson for aspiring business leaders—adaptation is the compass that navigates the journey to success.

The spirit of competition is deeply ingrained in the DNA of NFL players, and this spirit seamlessly translates to the world of entrepreneurship. The relentless pursuit of excellence that characterized their athletic careers finds a new canvas in the business arena. Challenges become opponents to conquer, and obstacles become opportunities for triumph. The drive to be the best is a universal language that transcends fields and fuels success in any endeavor.

## THE LEGACY BEYOND THE GAME

As the curtain falls on their NFL careers, these player-entrepreneurs embark on a new chapter—an entrepreneurial odyssey that extends their legacy beyond the boundaries of the game. The field of play may have shifted, but the pursuit of excellence remains unwavering. Their stories echo with lessons that span domains, resonating with aspiring business leaders who seek to carve their own path to success.

These gridiron success stories serve as a reminder that the essence of victory is multidimensional. Beyond the trophies and accolades, these individuals redefine triumph through adaptation, learning, and innovation. Their entrepreneurial journeys become the torchbearers of their legacy, illuminating industries, empowering communities, and inspiring those who follow in their footsteps.

In celebrating these journeys, we recognize that the playbook for entrepreneurship is a mirror reflection of the playbook for victory on the field. Both demand courage to tread uncharted territory, strategy to navigate uncertainties, and an unyielding commitment to excellence. The lesson is clear—just as an NFL player must master the nuances of the game to claim victory, an aspiring business leader must master the intricacies of entrepreneurship to claim their place at the helm of innovation and success.

# By: M.L. Ruscsak

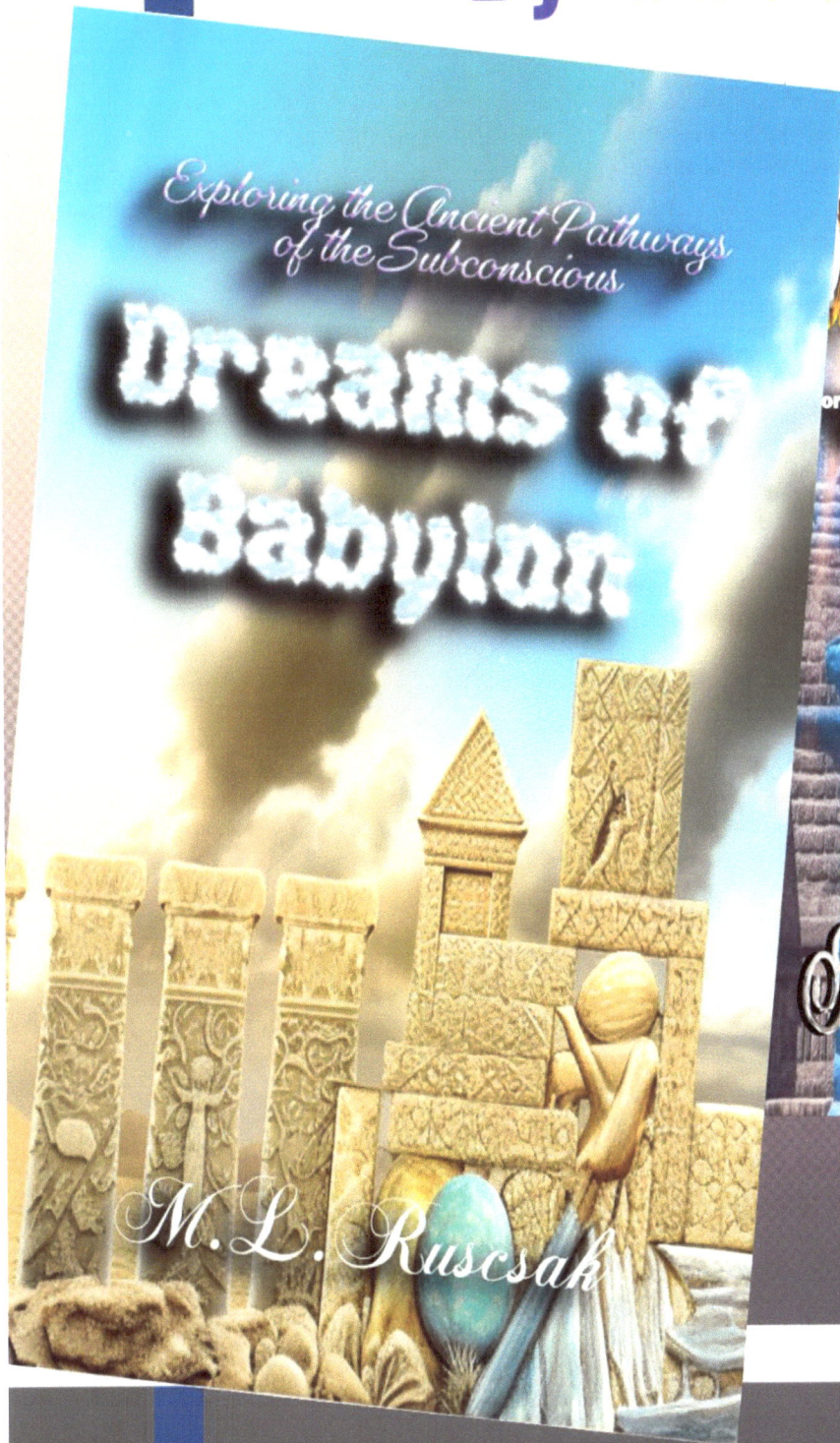

Exploring the Ancient Pathways
of the Subconscious

Dreams of Babylon

M.L. Ruscsak

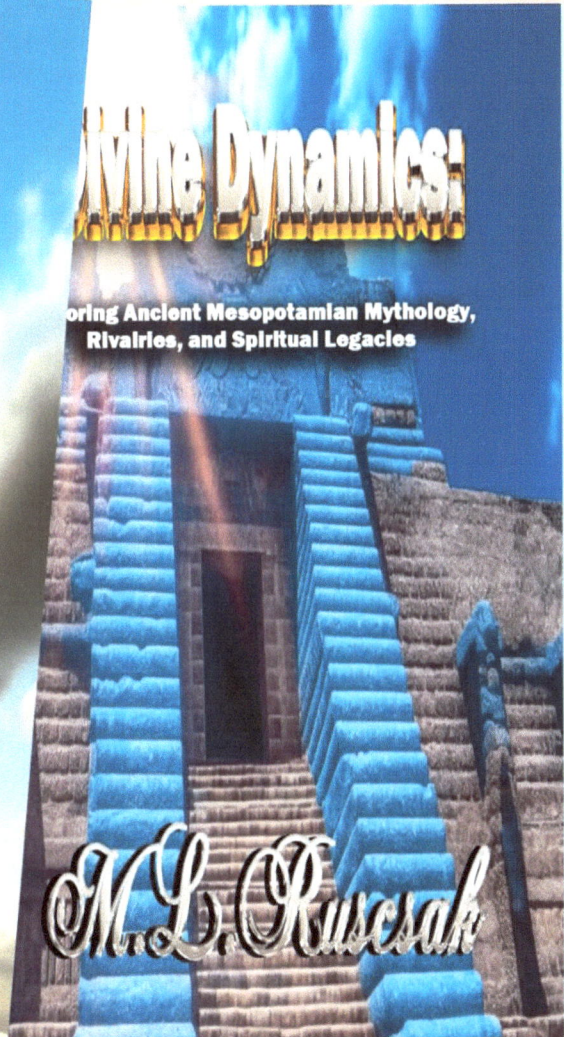

Divine Dynamics:

...loring Ancient Mesopotamian Mythology,
Rivalries, and Spiritual Legacies

M.L. Ruscsak

Trient Press®

# SCORING BIG OFF THE FIELD: BUSINESS VENTURES OF NFL LEGENDS

In the realm of professional football, where the gridiron serves as a stage for athletic triumph, a parallel narrative of victory is being etched—one that extends beyond the boundaries of the field and into the world of business. NFL legends, known for their athletic prowess, are proving that their capacity for success isn't confined to the end zones; it extends to the boardrooms, where they're charting new paths as business titans.

The transition from being a game-changer on the field to a game-changer in the business world is a journey that underscores the multifaceted nature of these individuals. Armed with the same drive, determination, and strategic acumen that earned them victories on game days, these NFL legends are venturing into the realm of business with an unwavering commitment to achieve excellence once again.

While their football careers remain an integral part of their identities, these NFL legends recognize the power of diversification. They're leveraging their status, expertise, and personal brands to delve into diverse industries—fashion, technology, finance, and more. This dynamic approach to business not only secures their financial futures but also extends their impact far beyond the gridiron.

The transition from athlete to entrepreneur isn't merely a shift in career—it's an embodiment of the MVP mindset. The qualities that earned them recognition as Most Valuable Players on the field are the same qualities that propel them to success in the business arena. From discipline to adaptability, from resilience to leadership, these attributes form the bedrock of their entrepreneurial endeavors.

However, the journey from the locker room to the conference room isn't just a change of scenery; it's a seamless transformation. The teamwork and camaraderie that defined their NFL careers now manifest in their business ventures. Collaborative strategies, effective communication, and the ability to build cohesive teams are skills that seamlessly transition from the turf to the corporate landscape.

These NFL legends aren't just venturing into business for personal gains; they're blazing trails for the next generation. By scoring big off the field, they're demonstrating to aspiring athletes that their journey doesn't end with retirement. Instead, it's a transition to a new arena of opportunity, where their determination and vision can lead to triumph once again.

In conclusion, the story of NFL legends doesn't culminate with their retirement from the field; it's a continuum of achievement, marked by victories in both the athletic and business realms. Scoring big off the field isn't just a financial feat—it's a testament to the enduring spirit of competition, innovation, and leadership that defines their essence. Their impact echoes not only in stadiums but also in boardrooms, where they're reshaping industries, inspiring new generations, and leaving an indelible legacy that transcends boundaries.

# COACHING FOR SUCCESS:

# LEADERSHIP LESSONS FROM NFL HEAD COACHES

In the dynamic world of professional football, where victory hinges on strategy, execution, and unwavering teamwork, the spotlight often shines on the players. But behind the scenes, orchestrating the symphony of triumph, are the unsung heroes—the NFL head coaches. These strategic masterminds don't just mold teams; they mold leaders. This article unveils the leadership lessons that NFL head coaches bring to the field, showcasing how their insights resonate far beyond the gridiron.

## Strategists of Success: The Coaching Playbook

From meticulously designed plays to agile game-time adjustments, NFL head coaches operate on a bedrock of strategy. This playbook for success transcends Xs and Os —it's a blueprint for effective leadership. Just as they devise plays to outmaneuver opponents, they deploy strategies to navigate complex challenges, inspire teams, and drive results. Their ability to craft a winning playbook translates into crafting a winning team culture.

### Strategizing Beyond the Sidelines

Discover how the playbook of NFL head coaches goes beyond Xs and Os, offering leadership insights that transcend the field.

### Leadership in Motion

Unveil the dynamic world of NFL head coaches as they orchestrate victories on and off the field, embodying the essence of strategic leadership.

### From Touchdowns to Triumphs

Explore how NFL head coaches transition their game-winning strategies into leadership blueprints, crafting champions in both sports and business.

## Leading by Example: A Touchdown of Trust

NFL head coaches understand that leadership isn't just about giving orders—it's about setting the bar high and leading by example. They embody the work ethic, dedication, and discipline they expect from their players. This authenticity fosters trust, creating a culture where commitment and accountability thrive. Just as players look up to coaches, employees look up to leaders who walk the talk.

## Game-Changing Communication: Inspiring from the Sidelines

The art of communication is a cornerstone of effective coaching, and the lessons here reverberate in the realm of leadership. NFL head coaches don't just bark orders; they communicate with precision, clarity, and motivation. Their ability to inspire players in the heat of competition mirrors the ability of leaders to rally teams toward shared goals. The power of well-crafted messages knows no bounds.

## Adapt or Be Defeated: Navigating the Playbook of Change

In the ever-evolving landscape of football, adaptability is non-negotiable. NFL head coaches pivot strategies based on the ebb and flow of the game. This adaptability is a lesson in agility—a quality that leaders must possess to thrive in a fast-paced business world. Just as coaches change tactics mid-game, leaders must adjust to changing market dynamics to stay ahead.

## Legacy of Mentorship: Coaching for Life

The mentorship legacy of NFL head coaches is a masterclass in leadership. They not only mold players into champions but also guide them on a journey beyond their athletic careers. This mentorship echoes in the business world, where leaders are entrusted with shaping the next generation. Just as coaches impart wisdom, leaders guide employees toward their full potential.

## Beyond the Sidelines

The lessons from NFL head coaches transcend football —they echo in the realm of leadership and beyond. Their strategies, communication prowess, adaptability, and mentorship offer invaluable insights for those striving to lead teams to victory. Just as NFL teams rally under their coaches' guidance, businesses thrive under the guidance of leaders who emulate these principles.

In the tapestry of leadership, NFL head coaches are the threads of inspiration that weave through both sports and business. Their playbook is more than a tactical guide; it's a testament to the qualities that drive success—strategic thinking, authenticity, communication, adaptability, and mentorship. As we celebrate the triumphs on the field, let's not overlook the invaluable playbook of leadership these coaches offer to those eager to lead their own teams to victory.

# GAME CHANGERS:

## *ATHLETES TURNED ENTREPRENEURS REDEFINING THE BUSINESS LANDSCAPE*

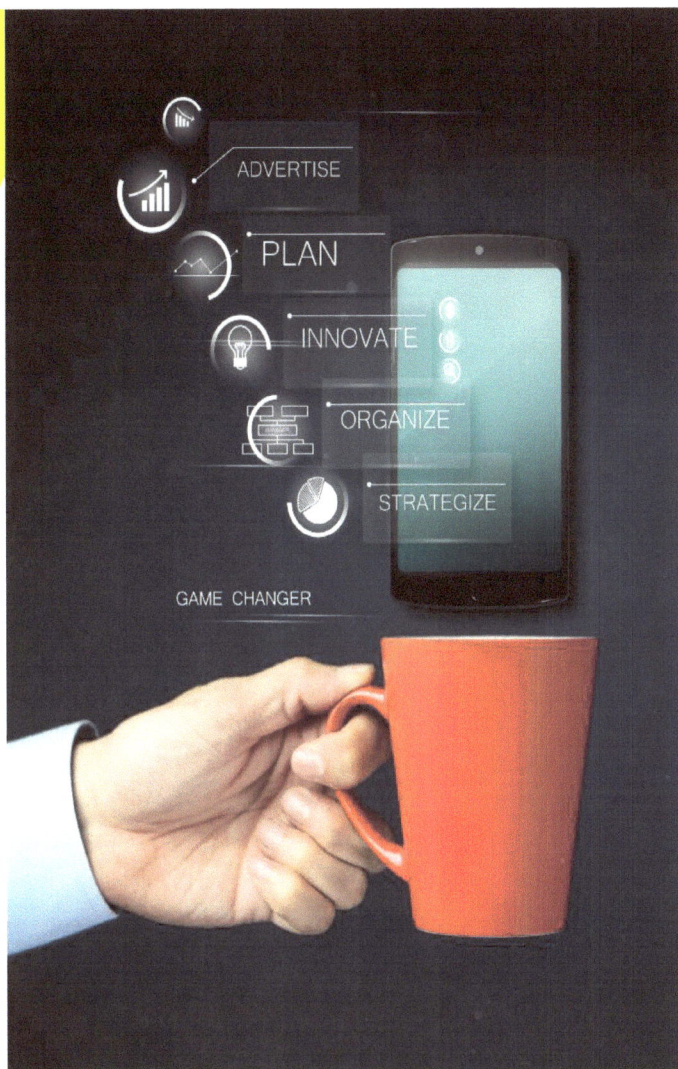

In the annals of sports history, tales of athletes dominating the field have long been celebrated. But what happens when these same athletes step off the turf and into the realm of business? A new narrative unfolds—a narrative of game changers who don't just thrive in one arena but use their prowess to redefine the business landscape. From slam dunks to startup successes, touchdowns to tech innovations, athletes turned entrepreneurs are crafting legacies that extend far beyond the scoreboard.

## The Pivot from Arena to Boardroom

When the final whistle blows on an athlete's sports career, a question looms large: what comes next? Many find the answer not on another playing field, but in the high-stakes arena of entrepreneurship.

The transition is more than a pivot; it's a reinvention —a transformation of a game plan into a business strategy. Take Kobe Bryant, the legendary NBA star. Post-retirement, he didn't rest on his laurels; he co-founded venture capital firm Bryant Stibel, using his winning mentality to identify and nurture startups.

## Transcending Sporting Glory

The story of athletes turned entrepreneurs isn't just about financial gains; it's about redefining legacies. Serena Williams, an unparalleled force in tennis, didn't stop at Grand Slam titles. She launched Serena Ventures, investing in a wide range of industries, from fashion to health tech. Her ventures aren't just diversifying her portfolio; they're reshaping her legacy as a multi-faceted influencer, innovator, and leader.

### From Locker Room to Tech Hub

The tech realm, often seen as the playground of engineers, is being transformed by athletes who've traded jerseys for startup tees. LeBron James, known for his slam dunks, made waves with his investment in Blaze Pizza. But his entrepreneurial foray didn't stop there; he co-founded SpringHill Entertainment, a media company, and Uninterrupted, a digital media platform. These ventures aren't just about financial gain; they're about carving a space for athletes in industries once considered distant from the sporting world.

### Crossover Success: Lessons from Athlete-Entrepreneurs

The playbook of athlete-entrepreneurs isn't just about winning; it's about resilience, adaptability, and the ability to face challenges head-on. Dwayne "The Rock" Johnson, famed for his wrestling and acting, took his winning mentality to the tequila business. He co-founded Teremana Tequila, showcasing that success isn't confined to one domain—it's a mindset that transcends industries.

### Inspiration Beyond Sports

The stories of athletes turned entrepreneurs are more than anecdotes; they're inspirations that permeate industries. Consider Chris Paul, known for his basketball prowess. He co-founded PlayersTV, a media platform that bridges the gap between athletes and content creation. His journey exemplifies that the tenacity that leads to championships can also lead to groundbreaking initiatives that reshape how we consume media.

### The Resonance of Transformation

In the realm of business, as in sports, transformation is the essence of success. Athletes turned entrepreneurs embody this principle, illustrating how the drive that fueled their athletic victories can seamlessly translate to business triumphs. Shaquille O'Neal, an NBA legend, ventured into diverse arenas from real estate to franchising. His transformation from court domination to business diversification underscores that versatility is the currency of success.

### Beyond the Game, into the Future

The tales of athletes turned entrepreneurs aren't just about financial acumen; they're about rewriting narratives. These game changers are proving that their victories don't end with championships; they're translated into influential ventures that redefine industries. As we celebrate their achievements, let's remember that the business landscape, much like the sporting arena, is shaped by those who dare to challenge conventions, embrace transformation, and redefine what it means to be a champion.

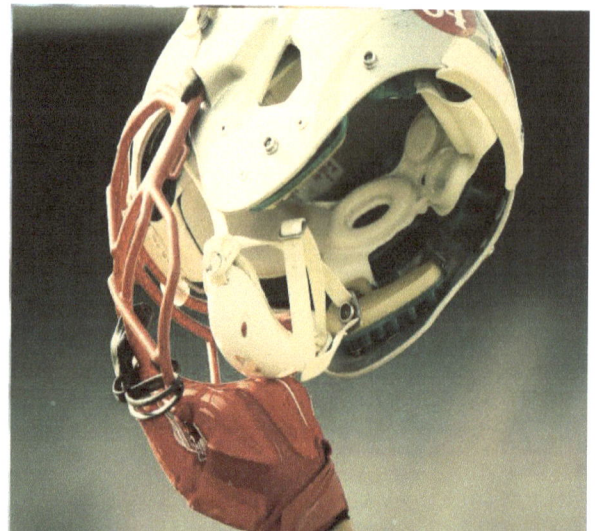

M.L. Ruscsak

MAKE THIS YEAR YOUR BEST YEAR

PODCAST
Your Way to Success

M.L. Ruscsak

Trient Press

# PRESS RELEASE

01 August, 2023        **For Immediate Release**

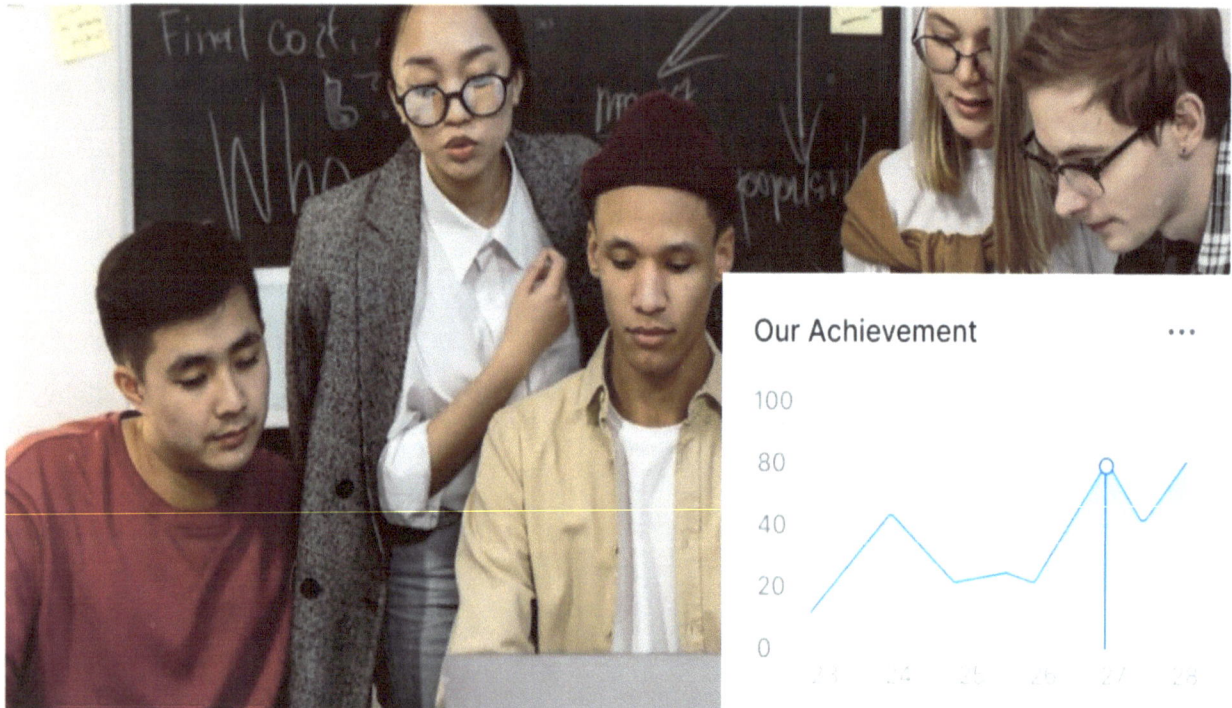

**Our Achievement**    ...

100
80
40
20
0

## AMPLIFY YOUR SUCCESS AND MAXIMIZE PROFITS WITH ATS LEADS

Imagine leveraging Google's vast public database, social media platforms, targeted hashtags, and precise email lists to connect with your prospective clients. Discover customers who are eager to buy from you. Tap into an abundant wealth of business opportunities with our precision targeting. Seize the moment, close lucrative deals, and watch your revenue skyrocket! 💼 💰

With us, you're not just unlocking leads. You're unlocking the path to exponential growth.

# In the Huddle: Collaborative Partnerships Between NFL Players and Brands

In the ever-evolving landscape of branding and marketing, a new playbook is being crafted—one that brings together NFL players and brands in collaborative partnerships that transcend traditional endorsements. Gone are the days of superficial sponsorships; today's landscape is marked by authentic alliances that resonate with audiences, create impact, and redefine the rules of engagement. In the huddle of these partnerships, the convergence of sports and business creates a symphony of resonance and opportunity.

## BEYOND ENDORSEMENTS: A PARADIGM SHIFT

THE TRADITIONAL MODEL OF ATHLETE ENDORSEMENTS WAS SIMPLE—A PLAYER ATTACHED THEIR NAME TO A PRODUCT AND COLLECTED A PAYCHECK. BUT THE GAME HAS EVOLVED. TODAY'S COLLABORATIONS ARE BUILT ON SHARED VALUES, MUTUAL GOALS, AND A DESIRE TO CREATE GENUINE CONNECTIONS. CONSIDER THE PARTNERSHIP BETWEEN NFL QUARTERBACK RUSSELL WILSON AND WEST2EAST EMPIRE. WILSON DIDN'T MERELY LEND HIS NAME; HE BECAME A STRATEGIC PARTNER, LEVERAGING HIS INSIGHTS TO DRIVE THE BRAND'S DIRECTION. THIS EVOLUTION UNDERSCORES THE PARADIGM SHIFT FROM SUPERFICIAL ENDORSEMENTS TO STRATEGIC PARTNERSHIPS.

## Crafting Authentic Narratives

In the huddle of collaborative partnerships, authenticity reigns supreme. Brands are seeking to tell stories that resonate with audiences, and who better to shape these narratives than the athletes themselves? Take the partnership between Dwyane Wade and Li-Ning, a Chinese sportswear company. Wade's active involvement in the design process and creative direction goes beyond a mere spokesperson role. It's a testament to the power of athletes as storytellers, and to brands recognizing their ability to craft compelling narratives.

Collaborative partnerships are also becoming vehicles for social change. NFL players, often regarded as influencers, are using their platforms to champion causes that matter. This goes beyond logo placements; it's about aligning with a shared mission. Colin Kaepernick's collaboration with Nike serves as a prime example. The "Just Do It" campaign didn't just celebrate athleticism; it championed social justice. The partnership wasn't just a marketing ploy; it was a statement of solidarity that resonated with a global audience.

## Experiences Beyond Products

In the huddle of these partnerships, experiences take center stage. Brands are realizing that consumers seek more than products; they crave experiences that enrich their lives. NFL players are uniquely positioned to provide these experiences. Take the partnership between Tom Brady and Aston Martin. Brady not only endorsed the brand but also co-created the Vanquish S Volante "Tom Brady Signature Edition." This partnership isn't just about a luxury car; it's about a unique experience woven into the fabric of Brady's story.

## Fan Engagement Amplified

Collaborative partnerships between NFL players and brands have a profound impact on fan engagement. These alliances become points of connection, fostering deeper relationships between players, brands, and fans. LeBron James' partnership with Coca-Cola serves as a case in point. Their collaboration extends beyond advertisements; it includes community initiatives and programs that resonate with fans who look up to James as a role model. This multi-faceted approach amplifies fan engagement and transcends mere product endorsements.

## Redefining ROI: Return on Impact

In the traditional realm of endorsements, ROI often referred to Return on Investment. But in the era of collaborative partnerships, it's becoming about Return on Impact. These partnerships redefine success, not just in terms of revenue generated, but in terms of impact created. It's about aligning brand objectives with athlete values and creating resonance that transcends marketing metrics. These partnerships amplify brand relevance, reshape cultural narratives, and enhance societal conversations.

## Beyond the Huddle, into the Future

The huddle of collaborative partnerships between NFL players and brands isn't just a trend; it's a fundamental shift in how the sports and business worlds intersect. As these partnerships reshape the marketing playbook, they invite us to imagine a future where authenticity, impact, and shared values define brand narratives. It's a playbook where athletes aren't just endorsers; they're creators, catalysts, and champions of change. But this transformation isn't without its challenges.

In the quest for authenticity, brands must be cautious of performative allyship or exploiting athletes' social stances for profit. The power of these partnerships lies in the alignment of values, where both parties genuinely advocate for a better world. As consumers become more discerning, partnerships that lack substance will not resonate. The future demands not just collaboration, but meaningful collaboration—one that rings true to both the brand's mission and the athlete's principles.

As we celebrate these innovative alliances, we're reminded that the game isn't just played on the field—it's also played in the hearts and minds of audiences around the world. The huddle of collaborative partnerships isn't just about marketing; it's about shaping culture, influencing conversations, and leaving a lasting impact. It's a dynamic arena where athletes and brands become co-creators of stories that transcend commerce and resonate with the human experience. As we peer into the future, we witness the birth of a new narrative—one where collaboration becomes the key to unlocking not only business success but also a better world.

# From End Zone to Boardroom: Transitioning Careers for Retired NFL Players

*M.L. Ruscsak*

"The journey of an NFL player is often lauded as a testament to dedication, skill, and the pursuit of excellence. But what happens when the roar of the crowd fades, and the stadium lights dim? The transition from the end zone to the boardroom is a narrative of resilience, reinvention, and the pursuit of new victories. Retired NFL players are rewriting the script of their lives, leveraging the skills honed on the field to thrive in the realm of business. This article delves into their stories, unpacking the challenges, strategies, and triumphs that accompany their career transitions.

Beyond the glory and adulation of their athletic careers lies a formidable challenge for retired NFL players: the transition to a new professional chapter. The camaraderie of the locker room, the adrenaline of the game, and the spotlight of fame all recede, leaving a void that must be filled with a new purpose. Moreover, the fast-paced, high-stakes nature of professional sports can be a difficult act to follow, as many struggle to find professions that offer the same intensity and competition.

Amidst these challenges, retired NFL players possess a treasure trove of transferable skills that can be wielded in new contexts. Leadership, teamwork, discipline, resilience, and adaptability are all skills that are second nature to athletes, and they form a formidable arsenal in the world of business. These skills, often forged in the crucible of competition, translate seamlessly into boardrooms, startup offices, and entrepreneurial endeavors.

Entrepreneurship is a common path for retired NFL players seeking to craft legacies beyond the field. The journey of players like Tony Richardson, who co-founded the "Rize" app to empower charitable actions, underscores the spirit of giving back instilled in many athletes. The transition to entrepreneurship not only creates financial opportunities but also offers a platform for philanthropic endeavors that echo their dedication to making a difference.

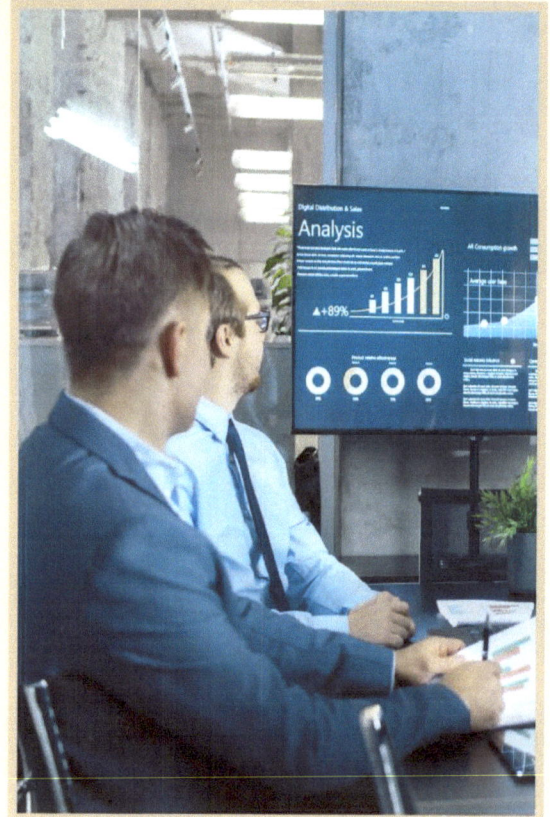

Networking is another facet where retired NFL players hold a distinct advantage. The relationships forged in the sports industry, from fellow players to team executives, form a vast network that can be leveraged in the business world. This interconnected community facilitates access to resources, mentorship, and opportunities that accelerate the transition process. Former NFL player Justin Tuck, for example, transitioned to a successful career in finance, leveraging his connections to create opportunities in a new field.

Transitioning from the NFL to the boardroom often requires a learning curve, and many players turn to education to bridge the gap. Pursuing advanced degrees, attending business seminars, and participating in training programs equip them with the knowledge needed for their new careers. The learning process is a testament to their determination to succeed in uncharted territories, embodying the same dedication that propelled them to excellence in football.

Retired NFL players who successfully transition to second careers become beacons of inspiration for current players and aspiring athletes. Their journeys underscore the importance of planning for life beyond sports, emphasizing the value of skills, education, and adaptability. Players like Peyton Manning, who transitioned from the field to business ventures and philanthropy, serve as living proof that success is not confined to one arena.

The transition from the end zone to the boardroom is an ongoing narrative—one that evolves with each retired NFL player who embarks on this journey. Their stories underscore the inherent ability to redefine oneself, the power of resilience, and the potential for success beyond sports. As we witness these athletes write new chapters in their lives, we recognize that their stories are not just about career transitions; they are about the indomitable spirit that propels human beings to excel, adapt, and create meaningful legacies beyond the confines of any field or stadium.

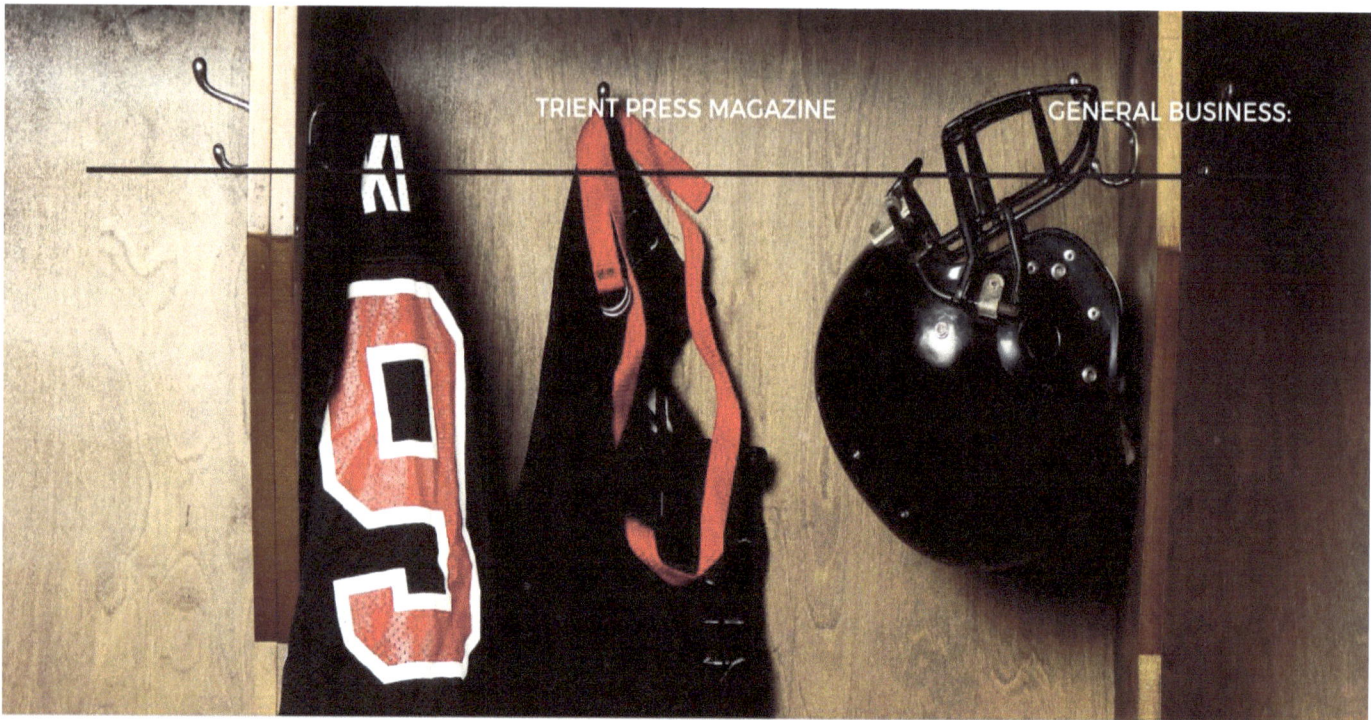

# Locker Room to Conference Room:

## Teamwork Lessons for Business Success

The echoes of success in the sports arena reverberate beyond the confines of stadiums, seeping into the fabric of business landscapes. The lessons distilled from the locker room, where teamwork forms the backbone of victory, translate seamlessly to the conference room, where collaboration propels business success. As the playbook of corporate dynamics evolves, the DNA of teamwork remains a timeless cornerstone. This article delves into the symbiotic relationship between teamwork on the field and collaboration in the business world, illuminating how the principles that underpin athletic triumphs form a blueprint for achieving greatness in the boardroom.

- **Synergy Beyond the Scoreboard: Collaborative Alchemy**

The locker room, an arena where diverse talents unite to chase a common goal, is a microcosm of effective collaboration. The shared objectives, unwavering commitment, and respect for individual contributions create a synergy that transcends individual capabilities. This collaborative alchemy, observed in championship-winning teams, reflects the essence of effective teamwork in business—a potent combination of expertise, dedication, and unity.

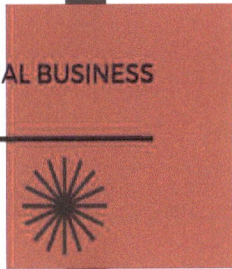

## Strategic Alignment: The Essence of Cohesion

Successful sports teams operate as harmonious units, with players strategically positioned to maximize their collective potential. This emphasis on alignment mirrors the business landscape, where strategic positioning of team members optimizes the overall performance. The synergy among players who comprehend their roles within the broader framework of the game draws a parallel with business units aligning their efforts towards common objectives.

## Resilience Under Pressure: Triumph Amidst Challenges

The crucible of sports breeds resilience, as teams endure setbacks and bounce back stronger. Adversity, a constant companion in the sports arena, mirrors the dynamic challenges faced in business. The ability of athletes to regroup, recalibrate, and continue pursuing victory imparts a crucial lesson—a resilient team thrives not only in times of triumph but also under the weight of challenges.

## Communication: The Pivot of Precision

In sports, communication is a linchpin that fosters coordinated strategies, swift decision-making, and seamless execution. This emphasis on effective communication resonates profoundly in the business realm, where information flow guides strategies, influences tactics, and navigates unforeseen obstacles. The shared language among athletes finds its parallel in the business context, where a well-informed team contributes to strategic precision.

## Leadership Dynamics: Captains on and off the Field

Sports teams often look up to captains for guidance, strategy, and inspiration. The parallels between these leadership dynamics and those in business are evident. Effective leaders, whether in the locker room or the conference room, galvanize their teams, set clear directions, and embody the principles they espouse. The captain's role extends beyond individual prowess—it's about fostering collective excellence.

- ## The Art of Delegation: Empowering Success

In sports, coaches delegate roles based on players' strengths and expertise. This nuanced approach to delegation mirrors the art of effective leadership in business. Entrusting team members with responsibilities that align with their proficiencies not only empowers them but also ensures that the collective effort is honed for maximum impact.

- ## Adaptation and Evolution: Learning from Defeat

In sports, losses serve as lessons in adaptation and evolution. Business encounters analogous scenarios, where setbacks illuminate paths for improvement. The resilience to learn from defeat and strategize for future victories is a shared trait between athletes and business leaders.

## A Symphony of Collective Success

The echoes between the locker room and the conference room extend beyond mere symbolism— they echo the enduring principles that anchor human accomplishment. As athletes and business leaders forge their narratives of triumph, the lessons of teamwork, strategic alignment, communication, resilience, and leadership converge to weave an intricate tapestry of achievement. The unity that propels athletes toward victory resonates harmoniously with the cohesion propelling businesses toward excellence. From locker rooms to conference rooms, the resonant symphony of teamwork persists, serving as a reminder that the pursuit of success, regardless of the domain, thrives on the collective synergy of dedicated effort, deliberate strategy, and an unwavering commitment to collaboration.

In both sports and business, the intricate choreography of collaboration shapes victories, whether on the field or in the marketplace. The synchronized efforts of athletes mirror the coordinated strategies of teams navigating complex business challenges. The interplay between strategic alignment and individual contributions, witnessed in the locker room, serves as a blueprint for corporate strategies that align talents toward common objectives. Moreover, the spirit of leadership demonstrated by captains translates seamlessly to the business context, underscoring the significance of inspirational guidance and adept decision-making.

As the journey from the locker room to the conference room unfolds, the symphony of shared lessons resounds, reminding us that the threads of achievement are woven through a tapestry of teamwork, resilience, and unwavering determination. Whether in the pulsating world of sports or the dynamic landscape of business, the echoes of collaboration reverberate—a timeless melody that continues to resonate across domains, redefining the boundaries of triumph and uniting athletes and business leaders in a common pursuit of excellence.

By: Tracey Armstrong

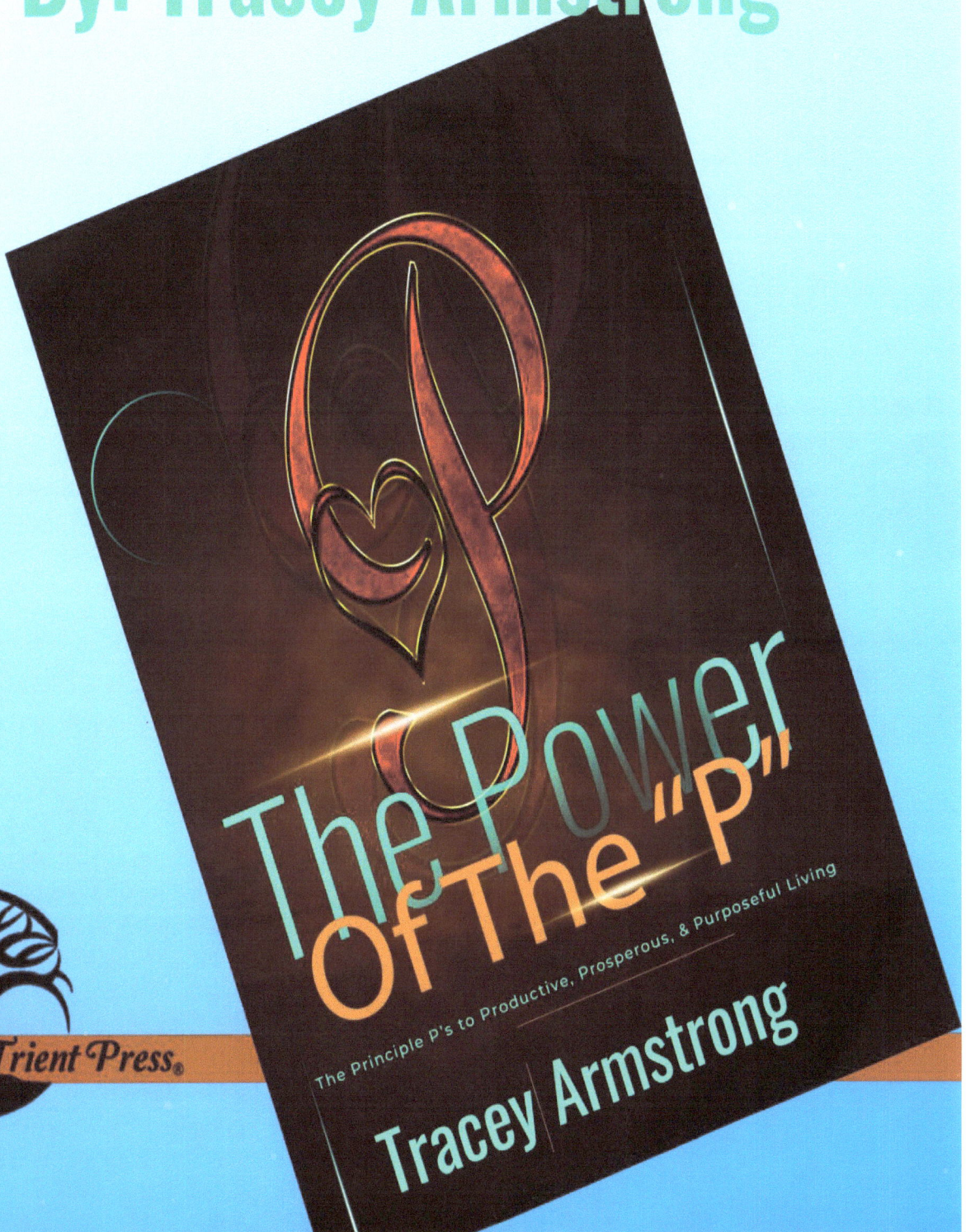

The Power of The "P"

The Principle P's to Productive, Prosperous, & Purposeful Living

Tracey Armstrong

Trient Press

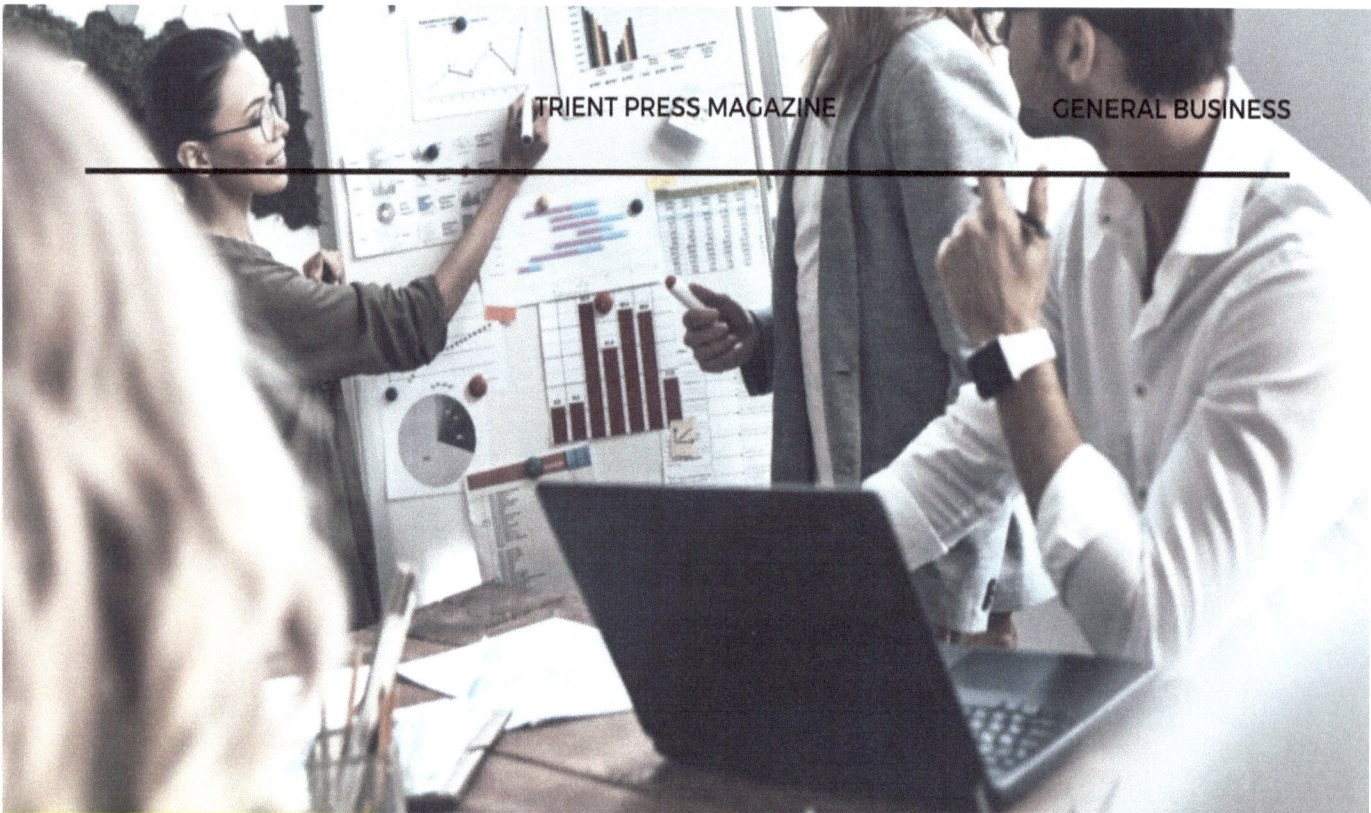

# INNOVATION ON THE FIELD AND IN BUSINESS:
## Tech Trends Influencing the NFL

In the realm of professional sports, where inches can define victories and split-second decisions determine outcomes, innovation is the heartbeat that propels both athletes and business leaders toward new horizons. The National Football League (NFL), an arena where tradition intersects with cutting-edge technologies, stands as a remarkable showcase of how tech trends can redefine the boundaries of competition and reshape industries. This article delves into the captivating narrative of how innovation, both on the football field and in the realm of business, converges into a symphony of transformation, sparking breakthroughs that transcend the confines of tradition and usher in an era of boundless possibilities.

### Technology as a Game Changer: Unveiling the NFL's Technological Evolution

In the pursuit of victory, the NFL has embraced technology as a game-changing ally. From the advent of instant replay to the marvels of virtual reality training, technology has propelled the league into new dimensions of competitiveness. Innovations like the Next Gen Stats, utilizing real-time player data, have not only elevated the spectator experience but have also become invaluable tools for coaches and strategists. The advent of wearable tech, monitoring player performance and health in unprecedented ways, epitomizes the fusion of tech and athletics, setting a precedent for how data-driven insights are transforming the landscape of sports.

# THE TECH-POWERED PLAYBOOK FOR BUSINESS SUCCESS

As technology transforms the NFL, its influence echoes far beyond the field, infusing business strategies with a new tempo of innovation. From AI-driven analytics reshaping marketing campaigns to blockchain revolutionizing supply chains, the tech trends that govern the business world find resonance in the playbook of the NFL. Just as coaches devise strategies to exploit opponents' weaknesses, business leaders leverage AI to anticipate market trends and consumer preferences. The collaborative dynamics of football teams inform corporate teamwork, and the spirit of agile adaptation embraced on the field becomes a blueprint for businesses navigating the dynamic landscapes of industry disruption.

## Tech-Tinged Futures: The Intersection of Athletics and Enterprise

The narrative of innovation in the NFL converges with that of business in a tapestry where tradition and technology intertwine. The pursuit of excellence in both domains hinges on harnessing the potential of emerging tech trends. The NFL's technological journey underscores that innovation transcends individual arenas—it's a universal language of progress. The lessons drawn from virtual training and real-time data insights, whether enhancing athletic performance or refining business strategies, highlight the interconnected nature of human endeavor. As technology continues to redefine the playbook, the echo of innovation resonates across industries, offering an exhilarating glimpse into the limitless possibilities when tradition meets transformation.

From the hallowed turf of the NFL to the bustling corridors of business, the narrative of innovation weaves a saga of evolution, resilience, and the human spirit's relentless pursuit of excellence. As athletes harness technology to push their limits, business leaders orchestrate their symphonies of transformation. In this intersection of athletic prowess and business acumen, we find an unceasing pursuit of advancement—a shared journey where innovation is the key to unlocking new horizons and redefining the very fabric of success.

# SCOUTING TALENT: HOW NFL PLAYER RECRUITMENT RELATES TO HIRING IN BUSINESS

"Recruitment and team building are essential in both sports and business. The success of any endeavor hinges on identifying the right talent, nurturing their potential, and fostering a culture of collaboration." - Kobe Bryant

In the high-stakes arena of professional sports, the process of scouting and recruiting talent is a meticulously orchestrated symphony—a dance of precision that brings together the best athletes to form a winning team. This ritual, laden with nuances and insights, isn't merely confined to the world of sports. Its echoes reverberate across the landscape of business, where the quest for exceptional talent lies at the heart of organizational success. In this exploration, we unravel the intriguing parallels between NFL player recruitment and the art of hiring in the corporate world, exposing the secrets that drive both realms toward excellence.

## The Draft Day and Onboarding: Cultivating Success from the Start

The NFL draft day, akin to the corporate onboarding process, marks the beginning of a new chapter—a juncture where talent is infused with opportunity. Teams invest in not just players' physical abilities but also their mental fortitude. Likewise, businesses invest in employees' potential, providing training, mentorship, and a conducive environment for growth.

## Cultivating a Winning Culture: Aligning Vision and Values

Perhaps the most resonant parallel between NFL player recruitment and business hiring lies in the pursuit of a winning culture. In sports, cohesive teamwork and a shared vision drive success. Similarly, businesses seek individuals who align with the company's culture and values, creating a collective force that propels the organization forward.

## Innovation and Adaptation: Lessons from Both Arenas

NFL scouting has evolved with technology, utilizing data analytics to unearth hidden gems. Similarly, businesses leverage AI and data-driven insights to forecast industry trends and make informed hiring decisions. Just as football teams adapt to dynamic game scenarios, businesses adapt to ever-changing market landscapes.

## A Shared Pursuit of Excellence

As we peel back the layers of NFL player recruitment and business hiring, a profound realization emerges: the pursuit of excellence is a universal endeavor, transcending sectors and industries. The recruitment process is more than a transaction—it's an investment in the future. Whether assembling a championship football team or a high-performing workforce, the principles of scouting, interviewing, onboarding, and nurturing a winning culture resonate across fields. In this synthesis of talent and vision, we uncover a harmonious symphony, where sports and business converge on the path to greatness.

## Unearthing Hidden Gems: The Science of Talent Identification

Much like NFL scouts pore over countless hours of game footage, scrutinizing every play and decision, businesses too comb through resumes and portfolios, searching for the right fit. In the realm of sports, the objective is to spot players who possess not just raw athleticism but also the potential to adapt, learn, and thrive within a team. Similarly, businesses seek individuals who bring not just technical skills but also a cultural fit and the ability to grow with the company

## The Art of Interviewing: Probing Beyond the Surface

The interview process in both the NFL and the business world mirrors a delicate dance of inquiry and assessment. In sports, prospects are probed about their decision-making under pressure, their ability to work within a team dynamic, and their capacity for resilience. Similarly, business interviews delve beyond the resume, exploring a candidate's problem-solving acumen, interpersonal skills, and compatibility with the company's values and goals.

MELISA RUSCSAK
EDITOR IN CHIEF

# NAVIGATING EXCELLENCE:

# BUILDING THE DREAM TEAM FOR TOMORROW'S MEDIA LANDSCAPE

**BY: KRISTINA WENZL-FIGUEROA**
VP & COO TRIENNIUM LYONS MEDIA, INTL
TRIENT PRESS, LYTRIONS FILM

In the ever-evolving landscape of media and entertainment, success hinges not only on innovation and vision but also on the people who drive it forward. As the Vice-President of an up-and-coming international media conglomerate, I am constantly reminded that our most valuable asset is our talented team. They are the architects of our success, the creative forces behind our content, and the beating heart of our organization.

In today's digital era, where the lines between media, technology, and content creation continue to blur, the pursuit of perfection in team composition is a never-ending quest. To maintain our position at the forefront of this dynamic industry, we must continually seek out individuals who not only possess exceptional skills but also embody the values and spirit of our company.

### The Essence of the Perfect Teammate

Before we embark on this journey to discover the ideal teammate, let's define what we mean by "perfect." In our context, perfection isn't about flawless individuals; it's about finding the right pieces to complete the puzzle. A perfect teammate is one who not only excels in their area of expertise but also seamlessly integrates into the culture and mission of our company. At our media conglomerate, diversity and inclusion are more than

"

*The secret to a successful hire is this: look for the people who want to change the world." – Marc Benioff, Salesforce CEO*

buzzwords; they are fundamental principles that guide our hiring decisions. We seek out individuals with diverse backgrounds, experiences, and perspectives because we understand that it is this rich tapestry of ideas that fosters innovation and creativity.

Additionally, adaptability and resilience are essential qualities in our ever-changing industry. Our perfect teammate is someone who thrives in ambiguity, embraces change, and views challenges as opportunities for growth. They are not content with the status quo but are driven to push boundaries and redefine what is possible.

### The Strategy of Recruitment

Finding the perfect teammate is not a task to be taken lightly. It requires a well-thought-out strategy that combines traditional recruitment methods with innovative approaches. Our recruitment process begins with a thorough evaluation of our company's goals and needs. What are the skills and attributes we require to meet the demands of our industry? What gaps exist within our current team?

Once we have a clear picture of our needs, we cast a wide net. We utilize online platforms, professional networks, and industry events to identify potential candidates. But our search goes beyond resumes and portfolios; we look for individuals whose values align with ours. Cultural fit is just as important as technical expertise.

### The Profound Impact

The impact of a perfect teammate on our organization cannot be overstated. They bring fresh perspectives that challenge the status quo, sparking innovation and creativity across the board. They inspire their colleagues to reach higher, to strive for excellence, and to embrace change as an opportunity rather than a threat.

Furthermore, a perfect teammate is a catalyst for collaboration. They bridge gaps between departments, fostering a sense of unity and shared purpose. Their presence enhances not only the quality of our work but also the workplace environment, making it more inclusive and vibrant.

In conclusion, as we journey through the ever-shifting tides of the media landscape, one thing remains constant: our reliance on the people who make up our team. Finding the perfect teammate is a journey filled with challenges and triumphs, but it is a journey that defines our success.

In our pursuit of excellence, we recognize that perfection is not an endpoint but a continuous endeavor. We must evolve with our industry, embracing change and diversity to remain at the forefront of media and entertainment. As the Vice-President of this media conglomerate, I am both honored and humbled by the dedication and passion of our team. Together, we will continue to navigate the complexities of our industry, driven by the knowledge that the perfect teammate is not a destination but a beacon guiding us toward a brighter future.

# PENNING VICTORY:
## CRAFTING COMPELLING NARRATIVES WITH NFL-INSPIRED STORYTELLING TACTICS

## From the Sports Perspective: The Anatomy of a Game-Changing Narrative

In the electrifying realm of sports, every match unfolds as a narrative—a dramatic story of skill, strategy, and triumph. The National Football League (NFL), a bastion of athletic prowess, epitomizes the art of weaving compelling narratives that captivate audiences around the world.

Each game isn't merely a physical contest; it's a saga of determination, rivalry, and the unyielding pursuit of victory. Much like a masterful storyteller, the NFL leverages storytelling tactics that keep fans on the edge of their seats.

### The Heroes and Villains: Characters That Ignite Passion

Every NFL game introduces protagonists—the teams—whose stories intertwine in a riveting clash of wills. Fans rally behind their chosen heroes, igniting a fervor akin to allegiance. Similarly, in the business world, brands become characters, each with its unique personality, values, and goals. Crafting a compelling narrative involves humanizing the brand, making it relatable and magnetic, much like the teams that inspire fervent loyalty on the field.

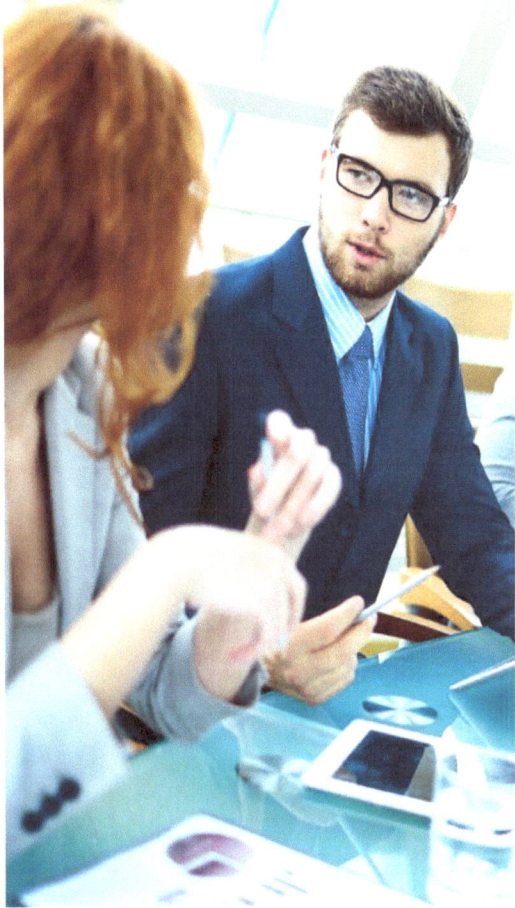

> **"Sports do not build character. They reveal it." - Heywood Broun**

### The Arc of Conflict: Drama That Drives Engagement

The tension that underpins an NFL game is a testament to the power of conflict. The ebb and flow of momentum, the unexpected turns of events—they're elements that elevate the narrative, fostering emotional investment. In business, creating narratives with conflict involves showcasing challenges and solutions, resonating with audiences who seek authenticity and relatability. Much like a team that overcomes adversity, a business that navigates obstacles inspires admiration and trust.

## THE GRAND FINALE: RESONANCE THROUGH RESOLUTION

A victorious ending in an NFL game is a cathartic release—an emotional payoff that resonates with fans. In business, narratives find resonance when they lead to a satisfying resolution—a transformational change, a breakthrough innovation, or a solution that addresses a pain point. The denouement is a moment of connection, where the audience celebrates the journey and its outcome.

## From the Business Perspective: The Art of Storytelling for Success

In the corporate world, storytelling is a potent tool that transforms brands into legends. Much like an NFL team's journey to the Super Bowl, businesses embark on a quest for success, and storytelling is their playbook.

### Defining the Narrative: Crafting a Unique Identity

An NFL team's narrative stems from its history, values, and aspirations. Similarly, businesses define their narratives by articulating their purpose, culture, and mission. A strong narrative becomes the cornerstone of brand identity, setting the stage for customer engagement and loyalty.

### Engaging the Audience: Eliciting Emotional Connections

The roar of the crowd at an NFL stadium is a testament to the emotional connection fans have with their teams. Businesses cultivate the same resonance by tapping into the emotions of their audience. Narratives that evoke empathy, excitement, or aspiration forge lasting connections, transforming customers into brand advocates.

> "Your brand is a story unfolding across all customer touch points." - Jonah Sachs

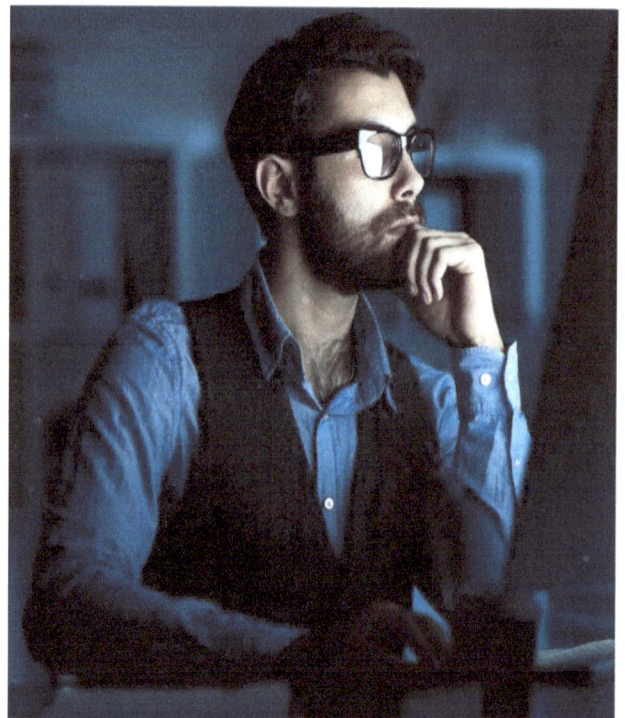

"People do not buy goods and services. They buy relations, stories, and magic." - Seth Godin

## Adapting and Evolving: Continuity in Change

An NFL team's narrative evolves with every game, adapting to new challenges and opportunities. Similarly, businesses must evolve their narratives to remain relevant and responsive to market shifts. The ability to pivot and reshape the narrative ensures an enduring presence in the minds of consumers.

## THE CONVERGENCE OF SPORTING SPIRIT AND BUSINESS SUCCESS

The parallels between NFL-inspired storytelling tactics and business narratives underscore the universal nature of storytelling. Whether on the field or in the boardroom, the art of crafting compelling narratives transcends domains, sparking emotion, engagement, and loyalty. As we celebrate the drama of sports and the dynamics of business, we recognize that at their core, both worlds are united by the power of a well-told story—one that captures the essence of triumph, the allure of conflict, and the resonance of resolution.

# End Zone to Bestseller List:

## *Touchdown Strategies Authors Can Borrow from NFL Playbooks*

In the riveting world of both sports and literature, the pursuit of success shares a common thread—the strategic pursuit of victory. The National Football League (NFL), renowned for its tactical prowess, serves as an unexpected source of inspiration for authors aiming to ascend the literary ranks. This article delves into the intersection of football and fiction, unveiling strategies from the NFL playbook that authors can adopt to propel their stories from the end zone of creation to the bestseller list.

### The Draft Strategy: Crafting Unforgettable Characters
In both football and literature, standout characters are the linchpins of success. Just as NFL teams meticulously scout players, authors must draft characters that resonate with readers. Develop layered personalities, aspirations, and conflicts that invite readers to invest emotionally in their journey, much like fans cheering for their favorite players.

### Game-Planning for Success: Plotting with Precision
The NFL thrives on game plans that exploit opponents' weaknesses. Similarly, authors must plot their narratives with meticulous attention to pacing, tension, and plot twists. A well-structured storyline keeps readers engaged, mirroring the edge-of-the-seat excitement of a football match.

### The Power of Collaboration: Assembling a Literary Team
In football, success relies on the collaboration of coaches, players, and staff. Authors can also benefit from a literary team, including beta readers, editors, and marketing experts. Their input and expertise refine the manuscript, ensuring a polished final product that resonates with readers.

### Adaptation and Flexibility: Navigating Plot Twists

Just as football games can take unexpected turns, narratives often evolve beyond the author's initial vision. Authors must adapt and pivot, responding to characters' choices and reader reactions. Embrace the unexpected, welcoming the creativity that arises from unexpected plot twists.

### The Super Bowl Moment: Crafting a Memorable Climax

The climactic moment of a football game is etched in history. Similarly, a well-crafted climax is the literary Super Bowl moment. Build tension and anticipation, then deliver a satisfying resolution that resonates with readers, leaving a lasting impact.

### Reviewing the Game Tape: The Editing Process

Post-game analysis is a staple in football; likewise, the editing process is vital for authors. Review the manuscript, refining prose, addressing plot holes, and fine-tuning dialogue. Like a successful post-game review, editing enhances the final product's quality.

### Honing Skills in the Off-Season: Continuous Learning

NFL players use the off-season to hone their skills; authors should engage in continuous learning too. Attend writing workshops, read widely, and explore new genres to expand your creative toolkit.

In the literary arena, as in football, success hinges on strategy, teamwork, and dedication. By borrowing insights from the NFL playbook, authors can score literary touchdowns that resonate with readers, solidifying their place in the league of celebrated storytellers.

# Drafting Success: Lessons from NFL's Team Building for Aspiring Author Alliances

Beyond the adrenaline-charged realm of professional football, where triumph is woven through coordinated teamwork, lies a wellspring of strategies that authors can tap into to draft their own literary success. The NFL's art of team building, the driving force behind the creation of winning teams, holds uncanny parallels to the world of aspiring authors seeking to shape alliances that propel their works to new heights. This article delves into the playbook of NFL team building, unearthing invaluable insights that resonate with authors aiming to draft success through strategic collaborations.

At the crux of both endeavors is the appreciation for complementary strengths. Just as an NFL squad is constructed with a mosaic of skills, authors can create alliances that blend their distinct talents, weaving together the narrative fabric with a diverse range of perspectives. Through this tapestry of abilities, the alliance produces works that are dynamic, nuanced, and rich in texture.

In the NFL, victory is rallied around a shared vision, and this holds true for authors as well. Crafting alliances that align with mutual aspirations and goals establishes a unified trajectory. It's a journey in which creativity finds its way into a harmonious synergy, as authors co-author novels, cross-promote their works, or collaborate on projects that kindle their artistic pursuits.

Just as NFL players receive constructive feedback from coaches, authors within alliances benefit from the same dynamic. The environment of collaboration fosters a safe space for sharing ideas and critique, ultimately nurturing the growth of manuscripts into polished, refined gems. Constructive criticism, served with respect and intention, becomes the whetstone that sharpens the narrative's edge.

Diversity is a cornerstone of NFL teams, each player contributing a unique piece to the puzzle. Likewise, authors aligned in an alliance bring their distinct experiences and perspectives to the table, enriching the storytelling process. Through this diversity, narratives emerge that are kaleidoscopic in depth, inviting readers into worlds they might not otherwise encounter.

In the NFL, roles and communication are key to coordinated play. Similarly, within the realm of author alliances, well-defined roles and open lines of communication ensure a seamless creative journey. Clear delineation of responsibilities minimizes misunderstandings, while transparent communication paves the way for productive collaboration.

In the enthralling interplay between the NFL's team-building prowess and the delicate artistry of literature, authors discover an unexpected convergence of strategies. By weaving insights from the NFL's playbook into the fabric of their own alliances, aspiring authors can unlock the potential of collaborative endeavors. In these alliances, the strengths of one are interwoven with the strengths of another, creating narratives that transcend the sum of their parts. It's a journey akin to drafting victory from the realm of teamwork, echoing triumphs of the gridiron on the pages of creative expression.

As authors set their sights on the limitless horizon of literary success, the parallels between the NFL's team-building strategies and the world of collaborative alliances become all the more evident. Just as football teams draft players to fortify their ranks and forge triumphant paths, authors can harness the power of alliances to elevate their own narratives to extraordinary heights. So, whether you're a seasoned writer seeking new avenues of collaboration or an aspiring wordsmith looking to embark on this exhilarating journey, remember the playbook of NFL team building. By embracing diversity, aligning visions, fostering communication, leveraging networks, and remaining adaptable, you too can draft a path to literary victory that resonates beyond the pages. The world of literature is waiting for the stories that only you and your collaborative allies can craft—so step onto the field of creativity, equipped with the wisdom of NFL-inspired strategies, and draft your own chapter of success.

From the world of football to the pages of literature, the power of networks remains pivotal. Just as NFL teams leverage connections to expand their reach, author alliances can tap into each other's networks, a feat that enhances visibility in an increasingly competitive literary landscape. The combined force of networks ushers in opportunities that may not have been accessible otherwise.

Victories, both on the field and in the realm of literature, are worth celebrating. In the NFL, triumphant touchdowns lead to exhilarating team celebrations. For authors, mutual accomplishments—book launches, awards, milestones—are cause for joint revelry. Shared success solidifies the alliance, infusing it with a sense of shared accomplishment and fostering an environment of mutual support.

Evolution is the heartbeat of NFL teams, who draft, trade, and adapt for sustained success. Likewise, author alliances must remain open to change, adaptable to new situations, and primed for growth as their collaborative journey progresses. As in the NFL, the realm of literature and creativity is not stagnant; it evolves and transforms, embracing the winds of change as the alliance forges its path forward.

# Traveling with Trient

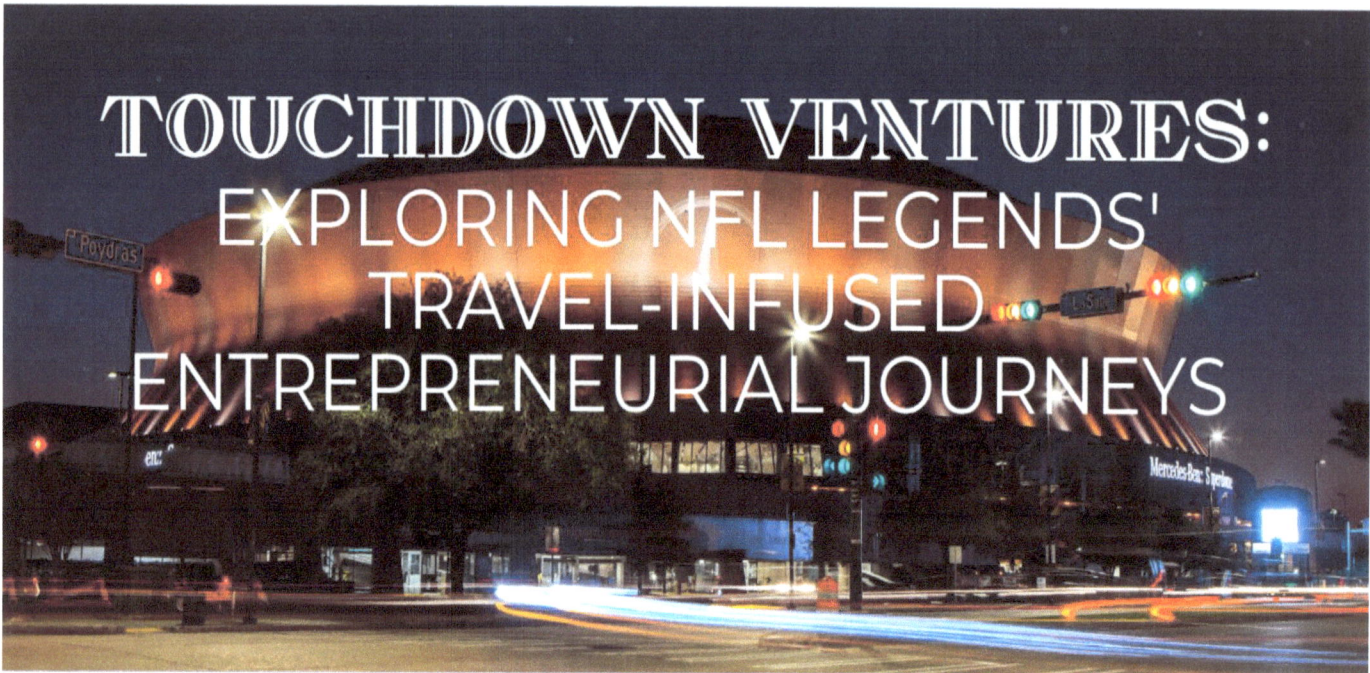

# TOUCHDOWN VENTURES:
## EXPLORING NFL LEGENDS' TRAVEL-INFUSED ENTREPRENEURIAL JOURNEYS

In the world of American football, the spotlight often shines brightest on the exhilarating moments that unfold on the gridiron. The adrenaline-pumping touchdowns, the game-changing tackles, and the electrifying victories command our attention and admiration. However, as a travel journalist and a fervent sports enthusiast, I invite you to embark on a unique journey—one that transcends the familiar boundaries of the field and delves into the travel-infused entrepreneurial endeavors of NFL legends.

Picture this: the same indomitable spirit and unwavering commitment that propelled these NFL stars to greatness on the field are now propelling them on a different kind of adventure—one that involves not just yards gained, but also miles traveled. The touchdowns of this venture are found not within painted end zones, but within the heart of novel experiences and unexplored horizons.

As we venture into the captivating narratives of these NFL legends turned travel-inspired entrepreneurs, an undeniable truth emerges. These remarkable athletes are not just trading their helmets for passport stamps; they're transitioning from a life of touchdowns to a life of touching down on new shores, where challenges and opportunities are as diverse as the landscapes they encounter.

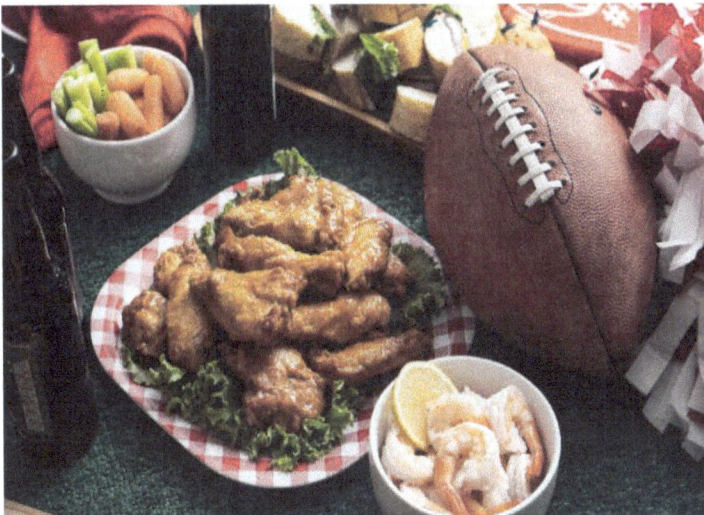

It's a league of wanderlust and innovation, where former NFL icons are channeling their passion for competition, their appetite for risk, and their dedication to excellence into new frontiers of entrepreneurship. Whether it's launching upscale restaurants in exotic locales or spearheading travel tech startups that cater to fellow wanderers, these legends are showcasing a versatility that extends beyond the football field.

Together, we'll journey through their stories—a compelling narrative that unfolds from the bright lights of the stadium to the bustling streets of distant cities. We'll uncover the threads that weave sports, travel, and business into a tapestry of unprecedented achievement. So fasten your seatbelts and get ready to embark on a touchdown venture that stretches beyond touchdowns themselves—an odyssey where passion, innovation, and the insatiable thirst for exploration converge. Through their inspiring experiences, these NFL legends are revealing that the pursuit of success isn't confined to a single arena—it's an ongoing journey that encompasses the world and the boundless possibilities it offers.

# ANTONIO T. SMITH JR.

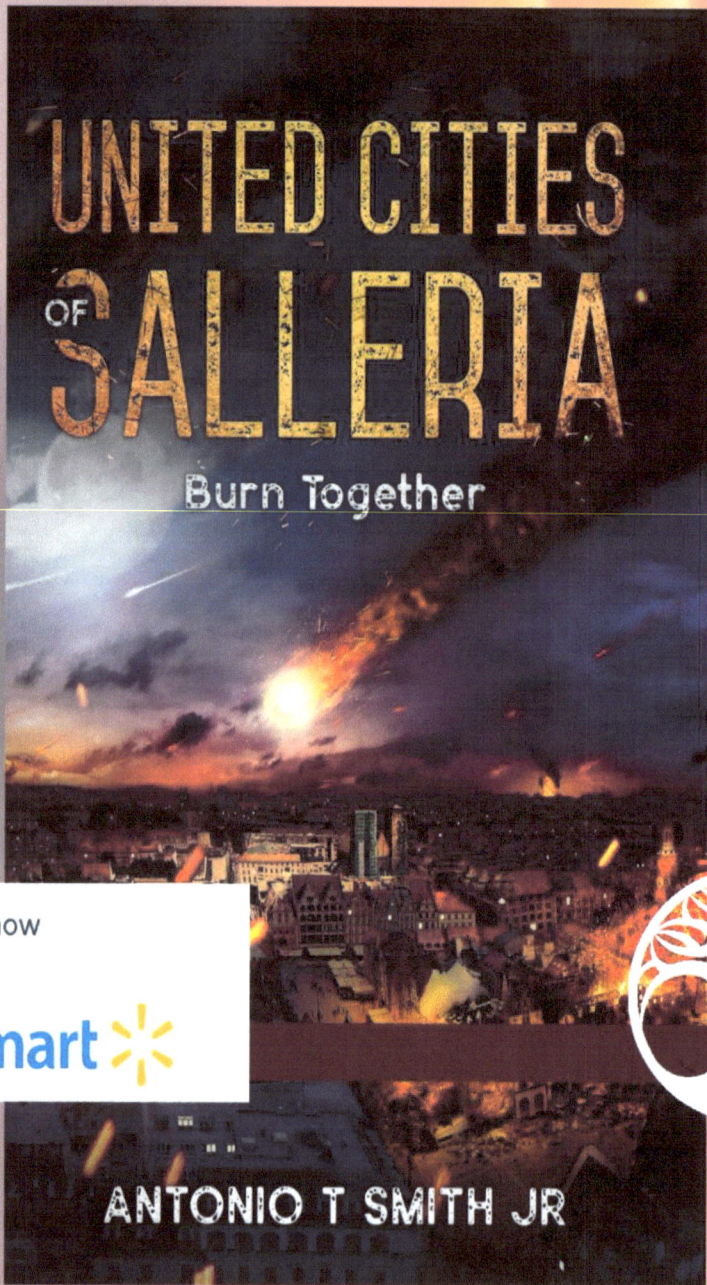

# GAME PLAN GETAWAYS:

## HOW NFL'S BUSINESS STRATEGIES *Inspire* TRAVEL INDUSTRY INNOVATIONS

*Blending Sports and Travel: Crafting Winning Journeys Inspired by NFL's Business Playbook*

By: M.L. Ruscsak

Dallas, Texas - In the heart of the Lone Star State, where the Dallas Cowboys proudly call AT&T Stadium their home turf, a unique convergence of sports and travel unfolds. As a travel journalist and an ardent NFL enthusiast, I find myself in Dallas to witness not only a thrilling game but also to delve into the ways in which the NFL's business strategies serve as a wellspring of inspiration for innovations within the travel industry.

The bustling streets of Dallas are abuzz with the excitement that only game day can bring. Fans from near and far descend upon the city, igniting a palpable energy that transcends the stadium walls. This dynamic, I can't help but notice, mirrors the travel industry's quest to create immersive experiences that go beyond mere transportation and accommodation. Just as the NFL strives to engage fans on and off the field, travel businesses endeavor to connect with travelers from the moment they step out their door.

> *"Where Sports and Wanderlust Unite: Exploring the NFL's Influence on Travel Experiences in Dallas, Texas"*

## A Tale of Fan Engagement and Brand Loyalty

The NFL's playbook of fan engagement is a treasure trove for the travel industry. From tailgating rituals that foster camaraderie to fan zones that celebrate the sport's heritage, the NFL knows how to create an environment that keeps fans coming back for more. Travel businesses, too, have adopted this playbook, curating experiences that immerse travelers in local cultures and narratives. Just as a die-hard fan proudly dons their team's jersey, travelers seek brands that resonate with their passions and values, forging a bond that transcends transactions.

As the game unfolds and the crowd erupts in cheers, I'm struck by the parallels between the NFL's pursuit of touchdowns and the travel industry's quest to create lasting memories. The joy of witnessing a game-winning touchdown mirrors the euphoria travelers experience when discovering a hidden gem in a foreign city. The NFL's ability to turn fleeting moments into lifelong memories resonates with travel's mission to transform journeys into stories that linger long after the adventure ends.

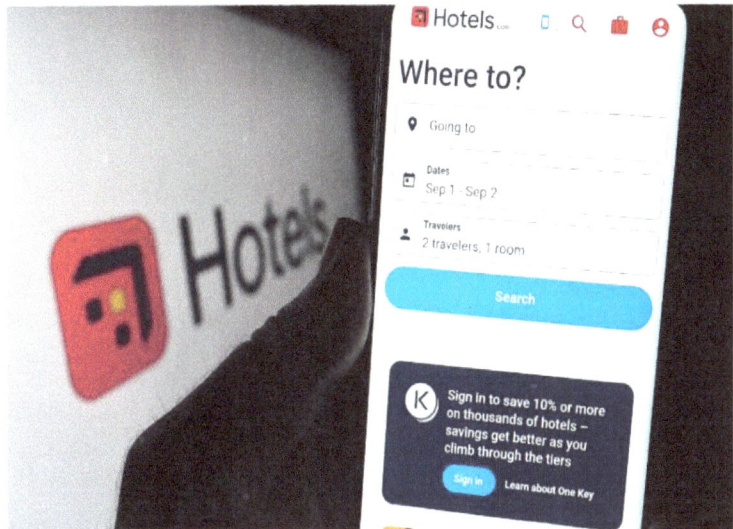

As the anticipation for the upcoming football season builds, I find myself reflecting on the echoes of past victories at the AT&T Stadium, home to the Dallas Cowboys. While the roar of the crowd and the thrill of the game are yet to fill the air, I'm already attuned to the remarkable parallels between the NFL's strategic prowess and the dynamic evolution of the travel industry. The dedication, teamwork, and innovation showcased by players on the field reverberate through the corridors of business, inspiring travel enterprises to craft experiences that allow adventurers to revel in their personal triumphs. This intricate interplay between the realms of sports and travel, carefully constructed through strategic planning and execution, weaves a narrative of mutual enrichment that propels both domains to unprecedented heights, leaving an enduring impact on enthusiasts and seekers of exploration.

# GLOBAL FANDOM: HOW THE NFL'S REACH SHAPES TRAVEL PATTERNS AND DESTINATION CHOICES

In the vast tapestry of international travel, the influence of sports is a thread that binds cultures, transcends borders, and unites people in shared passion. The National Football League (NFL), with its unwavering global fanbase, stands as a prime example of how sports can shape travel patterns and destination choices on a global scale.

From bustling metropolises to remote corners of the world, NFL fandom extends its reach, impacting the choices travelers make when venturing to new horizons. The phenomenon of "sports tourism" has gained momentum as avid fans strategically align their travel plans with major NFL events, such as the Super Bowl or international games. Just as travelers meticulously plan their itineraries to explore iconic landmarks, they now factor in sporting spectacles that hold immense cultural significance.

The NFL's ability to foster community and camaraderie among diverse fanbases amplifies its impact on travel. Fan associations, watch parties, and international fan clubs create networks that span continents, cultivating a sense of belonging that extends beyond game day. As fans gather to celebrate their team's victories or lament defeats, bonds are formed that motivate travel, enabling enthusiasts to meet face-to-face and share the euphoria of being part of a global tribe.

Moreover, the NFL's influence extends beyond the duration of games. Host cities of major events experience an economic influx as fans pour in, driving demand for accommodations, dining, transportation, and local attractions. This phenomenon ripples through the travel industry, showcasing the potential for sports to not only enrich cultural experiences but also boost local economies.

As travelers increasingly seek authentic and immersive experiences, the NFL's impact on destination choices becomes evident. Exploring a city during game week offers an alternative perspective, where the fervor of fans merges with the pulse of local life. Iconic landmarks, historic neighborhoods, and culinary gems all take on a new dimension as the energy of the game infuses the atmosphere.

The NFL's influence on travel patterns and destination choices is a testament to the power of sports as a cultural force. From uniting fans across continents to influencing travel decisions that shape economies, the NFL's global fandom has woven itself into the fabric of the travel industry. As travelers seek experiences that resonate with their passions, the intersection of sports and travel continues to carve unique pathways of exploration and connection on a global scale.

Now, let's delve into two exceptional hotels that not only cater to travelers but also cater to the fervent NFL enthusiasts in their own distinct ways—The Fairmont hotel in downtown Dallas, Texas, and The Clancy hotel in San Francisco. These reviews shed light on how these accommodations embody the spirit of sportsmanship, providing unique experiences that seamlessly blend hospitality and the thrill of NFL games.

# EMBRACING ELEGANCE:

## THE FAIRMONT HOTEL EXPERIENCE IN DOWNTOWN DALLAS

Nestled in the heart of downtown Dallas, just a stone's throw away from the vibrant Klyde Warren Park, the Fairmont Hotel stands as a beacon of sophistication and luxury. As a travel enthusiast and keen observer of impeccable hospitality, I had the privilege of experiencing the Fairmont firsthand during my recent visit to Dallas, Texas.

From the moment I stepped into the lobby, I was greeted with an ambiance that seamlessly blended modern elegance with a warm, welcoming atmosphere. The tastefully curated décor exuded a sense of timeless class, making it clear that attention to detail is a hallmark of the Fairmont experience.

My accommodations were nothing short of exceptional. The room, thoughtfully designed to cater to every need of a discerning traveler, boasted panoramic views of the city skyline that left me in awe. The blend of contemporary design elements and plush furnishings created a haven of comfort, inviting me to unwind after a day of exploring the city.

One of the standout features of the Fairmont is its commitment to culinary excellence. I indulged in a culinary journey at one of its renowned restaurants, where the fusion of flavors, artfully presented dishes, and impeccable service were a testament to the dedication of the hotel's culinary team. Whether savoring international cuisine or relishing local specialties, each meal was an experience that left an indelible mark on my palate.

The Fairmont's proximity to Klyde Warren Park added an extra layer of convenience and charm to my stay. A leisurely stroll through the park, enjoying live music and cultural events, was the perfect way to immerse myself in the vibrant spirit of downtown Dallas. The hotel's strategic location truly allows guests to embrace the city's offerings with ease.

Beyond its physical attributes, what truly sets the Fairmont apart is its commitment to delivering personalized service that goes above and beyond. Every staff member I encountered was attentive, accommodating, and genuinely invested in ensuring my stay was memorable.

As I reflect on my experience at the Fairmont Hotel in downtown Dallas, it's clear that this establishment embodies the essence of luxury, comfort, and authenticity. It's a haven where impeccable service, breathtaking views, and an unbeatable location converge to create an unforgettable travel experience.

Whether you're seeking a destination for business or leisure, the Fairmont stands as a testament to the art of hospitality and is a true gem in the heart of the city.

During my recent exploration of San Francisco, a city renowned for its iconic landmarks and vibrant energy, I had the pleasure of experiencing the exceptional hospitality of The Clancy hotel. As a sports enthusiast with a particular fondness for the NFL, I couldn't help but appreciate the strategic location of this superb establishment, especially for those planning to attend a thrilling 49ers game day.

Nestled in the heart of San Francisco's dynamic South of Market (SoMa) district, The Clancy offers a seamless blend of modern luxury and urban charm. The hotel's proximity to Levi's Stadium, the proud home of the San Francisco 49ers, is undoubtedly a standout feature for any football fan planning to catch a game. A short journey from the hotel to the stadium ensures that you're perfectly positioned to immerse yourself in the electric atmosphere of game day festivities.

# TOUCHDOWN HAVEN:

## THE CLANCY HOTEL~ YOUR ULTIMATE STAY FOR 49ERS GAMEDAY IN SAN FRANCISCO

Upon entering The Clancy, I was greeted by an ambiance that exuded contemporary elegance, with a nod to the city's rich history. The thoughtfully designed interiors seamlessly combined comfort and style, providing a welcoming respite after a day of exploring San Francisco's treasures.

My stay at The Clancy was a delightful experience from start to finish. The well-appointed room offered a panoramic view of the cityscape that was particularly enchanting during the evening hours. The attention to detail in the room's design and amenities spoke volumes about the hotel's commitment to providing a memorable stay.

The Clancy's dedication to culinary excellence was evident in its diverse dining options. Whether enjoying a sumptuous breakfast before a game-packed day or indulging in a sophisticated evening meal, every dish was a testament to the culinary team's skill and creativity.

What truly sets The Clancy apart is its strategic location for avid 49ers fans. The anticipation of game day was amplified as I ventured from the hotel to Levi's Stadium, surrounded by fellow enthusiasts sharing in the excitement. The convenience of being minutes away from the stadium added an extra layer of anticipation, ensuring I was part of the pre-game buzz.

From the moment I stepped into The Clancy, I was enveloped in an atmosphere of genuine warmth and hospitality. The friendly staff went above and beyond to ensure that every aspect of my stay was flawless. From assisting with recommendations for exploring the city to promptly addressing any requests I had, their dedication to guest satisfaction was truly commendable.

The Clancy's commitment to excellence extended to its facilities and amenities. The attention to detail was evident in every corner, from the elegantly designed common spaces to the well-appointed rooms that provided a harmonious blend of comfort and sophistication. The inviting ambiance of the hotel served as a soothing retreat after a day of vibrant city exploration.

What truly stood out was The Clancy's status as more than just a place to rest. It was an integral part of the San Francisco experience, especially for those attending a 49ers game day. The proximity to Levi's Stadium created a seamless connection between the hotel and the electrifying energy of the game. As I journeyed from the hotel to the stadium, the camaraderie among fellow fans and the shared excitement created an unforgettable prelude to the game itself.

For any sports enthusiast, The Clancy is not merely a stay—it's an immersion into the heart of the San Francisco 49ers fan culture. The hotel's strategic location, combined with its impeccable service and refined accommodations, solidified its position as a true companion for an unparalleled visit to the city and an exhilarating 49ers game day. From the anticipation in the air to the cheer of the crowd, The Clancy adds an extra layer of excitement to the journey, creating memories that linger long after the final whistle.

# MOUTH WATERING RECIPES

INTRODUCING THE "COWBOY'S PRIDE RIBEYE" - A DELECTABLE TOUCHDOWN OF FLAVORS!

Drawing inspiration from the spirit of the Dallas Cowboys and the vibrant culinary scene of Texas, the "Cowboy's Pride Ribeye" is a true NFL-inspired entrée that encapsulates the essence of both sports and local cuisine. This mouthwatering creation pays homage to the team's dedication and passion, delivering a winning combination of bold flavors and hearty satisfaction.

Starting with a premium, well-marbled ribeye steak, this entrée captures the essence of Texas barbecue with a savory dry rub that includes a blend of smoky paprika, zesty cumin, and aromatic garlic powder. The steak is then slow-cooked to perfection, allowing the flavors to meld and infuse every bite.

But what truly elevates the "Cowboy's Pride Ribeye" is the touchdown-worthy finishing touch—a rich and robust barbecue glaze infused with locally sourced ingredients.

This glaze, reminiscent of the fiery spirit of the game, combines sweet molasses, tangy tomato, and a hint of spicy chipotle for a harmonious balance of flavors.

Served alongside a duo of Texas-style roasted vegetables and a generous helping of garlic mashed potatoes, this entrée creates a culinary journey that mirrors the excitement of an NFL match. As you savor each tender bite of the "Cowboy's Pride Ribeye," you're transported to the heart of Texas, where the passion for football and the love for mouthwatering cuisine collide.

Whether enjoyed in the comfort of your own home or at a local restaurant, the "Cowboy's Pride Ribeye" is more than just a meal—it's an experience that brings the thrill of the game to your plate. So gather your fellow fans, fire up the grill, and embark on a culinary touchdown celebration that pays tribute to the iconic Dallas Cowboys and the irresistible flavors of the Lone Star State.

# Cowboy's Pride Ribeye

## INGREDIENTS

### FOR THE DRY RUB:

- 1 TABLESPOON SMOKED PAPRIKA
- 1 TEASPOON GROUND CUMIN
- 1 TEASPOON GARLIC POWDER
- 1 TEASPOON ONION POWDER
- 1 TEASPOON BROWN SUGAR
- 1/2 TEASPOON BLACK PEPPER
- 1/2 TEASPOON SALT
- 1/4 TEASPOON CAYENNE PEPPER (ADJUST TO TASTE)

### FOR THE SIDES:

- TEXAS-STYLE ROASTED VEGETABLES (SUCH AS BELL PEPPERS, ONIONS, AND CORN)

### GARLIC MASHED POTATOES

- 4 LARGE RUSSET POTATOES, PEELED AND CUBED
- 4-5 CLOVES OF GARLIC, MINCED
- 1/2 CUP HEAVY CREAM
- 4 TABLESPOONS UNSALTED BUTTER
- SALT AND PEPPER TO TASTE
- CHOPPED FRESH CHIVES OR PARSLEY FOR GARNISH (OPTIONAL)

### FOR THE RIBEYE:

- 2 BONE-IN RIBEYE STEAKS (ABOUT 1 INCH THICK)
- OLIVE OIL, FOR BRUSHING

### FOR THE BARBECUE GLAZE:

- 1/2 CUP KETCHUP
- 2 TABLESPOONS MOLASSES
- 2 TABLESPOONS APPLE CIDER VINEGAR
- 1 TABLESPOON BROWN SUGAR
- 1 TABLESPOON WORCESTERSHIRE SAUCE
- 1 TEASPOON DIJON MUSTARD
- 1 TEASPOON CHIPOTLE POWDER (ADJUST TO TASTE)
- SALT AND PEPPER, TO TASTE

IN A SMALL SAUCEPAN, HEAT THE HEAVY CREAM AND MINCED GARLIC OVER LOW HEAT. LET THE MIXTURE SIMMER GENTLY FOR A FEW MINUTES, ALLOWING THE GARLIC TO INFUSE THE CREAM.

MASH THE DRAINED POTATOES USING A POTATO MASHER OR A POTATO RICER. ADD THE BUTTER TO THE MASHED POTATOES AND MIX UNTIL THE BUTTER IS MELTED AND INCORPORATED.

GRADUALLY POUR IN THE WARMED GARLIC-INFUSED HEAVY CREAM WHILE CONTINUING TO MASH THE POTATOES. THE CREAM WILL ADD RICHNESS AND FLAVOR TO THE MASHED POTATOES. KEEP MASHING UNTIL YOU ACHIEVE YOUR DESIRED LEVEL OF CREAMINESS.

SEASON THE MASHED POTATOES WITH SALT AND PEPPER TO TASTE. REMEMBER THAT THE SEASONING CAN VARY BASED ON PERSONAL PREFERENCE, SO START WITH A LITTLE AND ADJUST AS NEEDED.

ONCE THE MASHED POTATOES ARE CREAMY AND WELL COMBINED, REMOVE THE POT FROM THE HEAT.

# Cowboy's Pride Ribeye

## DIRECTIONS

**Prepare the Dry Rub:**
- In a small bowl, combine all the dry rub ingredients. Mix well to ensure even distribution of spices. Set aside.

**Season the Ribeye:**
- Pat the ribeye steaks dry with paper towels. Brush both sides of each steak with a thin layer of olive oil. Sprinkle the dry rub generously over both sides of the steaks, pressing the rub into the meat to adhere.

**Grill the Ribeye:**
- Preheat the grill to medium-high heat. Place the ribeye steaks on the grill and cook for about 4-5 minutes on each side for medium-rare, or adjust the cooking time based on your desired doneness. During the last few minutes of grilling, brush the steaks with the barbecue glaze on both sides, allowing it to caramelize.

**Prepare the Barbecue Glaze:**
- In a small saucepan, combine all the barbecue glaze ingredients. Bring to a simmer over medium heat and cook for 5-7 minutes, stirring occasionally, until the glaze thickens. Remove from heat and set aside.

**Roast the Vegetables:**
- While the steaks are grilling, you can roast the Texas-style vegetables on the grill or in the oven. Toss the vegetables with a bit of olive oil, salt, and pepper. Grill or roast until they are tender and slightly charred.

**Serve:**
- Once the ribeye steaks are cooked to your preferred doneness, remove them from the grill and let them rest for a few minutes. Serve the ribeye steaks with a drizzle of the remaining barbecue glaze, alongside the roasted vegetables and garlic mashed potatoes.

# 49ers Gold Rush Burger

## Ingredients

### For the Burger Patties:

1 pound ground beef (80% lean)
1/2 teaspoon salt
1/4 teaspoon black pepper
1/4 teaspoon garlic powder
1/4 teaspoon onion powder
1/4 teaspoon smoked paprika

### For the Toppings:

4 hamburger buns
4 slices cheddar cheese
1 avocado, sliced
1 cup shredded lettuce
1 medium tomato, sliced
1/2 red onion, thinly sliced
Pickles

### For the Special Sauce:

1/2 cup mayonnaise
2 tablespoons ketchup
1 tablespoon yellow mustard
1 tablespoon sweet pickle relish
1 teaspoon white vinegar
1 teaspoon sugar
1/4 teaspoon onion powder
1/4 teaspoon garlic powder
Salt and pepper to taste

## Directions

In a bowl, combine the ground beef, salt, black pepper, garlic powder, onion powder, and smoked paprika. Mix gently to combine, being careful not to overwork the meat. Divide the mixture into four equal portions and shape them into burger patties.

Preheat a grill or stovetop skillet over medium-high heat. Cook the burger patties for about 3-4 minutes per side, or until they reach your desired level of doneness. During the last minute of cooking, add a slice of cheddar cheese to each patty and let it melt.

While the patties are cooking, prepare the special sauce. In a small bowl, whisk together the mayonnaise, ketchup, yellow mustard, sweet pickle relish, white vinegar, sugar, onion powder, and garlic powder. Season with salt and pepper to taste. Set aside.

Toast the hamburger buns on the grill or in a toaster until they are lightly golden and crisp.

## Directions Continued

Assemble the burgers: Spread a generous amount of the special sauce on the bottom half of each toasted bun. Place a cooked burger patty with melted cheese on top of the sauce.

Layer the burger with sliced avocado, shredded lettuce, tomato slices, red onion, and pickles.

Top the burger with the other half of the toasted bun, completing the masterpiece.

Serve the 49ers Gold Rush Burger with a side of your favorite fries, chips, or even some crispy onion rings.

This 49ers Gold Rush Burger captures the essence of San Francisco's football spirit while offering a hearty and flavorful burger experience. The combination of savory burger patties, creamy avocado, and tangy special sauce creates a taste sensation that's sure to delight both NFL fans and food enthusiasts alike. Enjoy this burger creation while cheering on your favorite team or whenever you're craving a satisfying meal with a San Francisco twist!

www.ingramcontent.com/pod-product-compliance
Lightning Source LLC
Chambersburg PA
CBHW050917210326
41597CB00003B/129